HSOAC
HOMELAND SECURITY
OPERATIONAL ANALYSIS CENTER

Developing Metrics and Scoring Procedures to Support Mitigation Grant Program Decisionmaking

JOSHUA MENDELSOHN, GRANT JOHNSON, KELLY KLIMA,
RACHEL STERATORE, SAMANTHA COHEN, GEOFFREY KIRKWOOD,
LLOYD DIXON, JAIME L. HASTINGS, PAUL S. STEINBERG

Published in 2021

Preface

This project developed metrics to support the Building Resilient Infrastructure and Communities (BRIC) Pre-Disaster Mitigation Grant Program. In consultation with program leadership, the Homeland Security Operational Analysis Center (HSOAC) divided the work into three lines of effort (LoEs), each of which produced metrics and/or assessment frameworks that can inform BRIC decisionmaking and performance evaluation. The findings should be of interest to those who work to make communities more resilient to natural disasters or to those who fund such work.

This research was sponsored by the Federal Emergency Management Agency (FEMA) and conducted within the Acquisition and Development Program of HSOAC, a federally funded research and development center (FFRDC).

About the Homeland Security Operational Analysis Center

The Homeland Security Act of 2002 (Section 305 of Public Law 107-296, as codified at 6 U.S.C. 185), authorizes the secretary of Homeland Security, acting through the undersecretary for science and technology, to establish one or more FFRDCs to provide independent analysis of homeland security issues. The RAND Corporation operates HSOAC as an FFRDC for the U.S. Department of Homeland Security (DHS) under contract HSHQDC-16-D-00007.

The HSOAC FFRDC provides the government with independent and objective analyses and advice in core areas important to the department in support of policy development, decisionmaking, alternative approaches, and new ideas on issues of significance. The HSOAC FFRDC also works with and supports other federal, state, local, tribal, and public- and private-sector organizations that make up the homeland security enterprise. The HSOAC FFRDC's research is undertaken by mutual consent with DHS and is organized as a set of discrete tasks. This report presents the results of research and analysis conducted under 70FA4018F00000128, Requirements Analysis and Specifications for FEMA.

The results presented in this report do not necessarily reflect official DHS opinion or policy.

For more information on HSOAC, see www.rand.org/hsoac. For more information on this publication, see www.rand.org/t/RRA377-1.

Contents

Figures and Tables

Figures

Tables

Summary

Introduction

The Robert T. Stafford Disaster Relief and Emergency Assistance Act (henceforth, the "Stafford Act") provides the key legal foundation for federal disaster response and recovery assistance activities. Section 1234 of the Disaster Recovery Reform Act of 2019 (DRRA) amends Section 203 of the Stafford Act. It emphasizes the importance of public infrastructure, building codes, cost-effectiveness, resilience, and targeting places where disaster declarations have occurred in the last seven years. It also adjusts the way that grant programs are funded, such that there is now up to 6 percent of certain disaster response/recovery spending estimates set aside from each disaster. In response, the Federal Emergency Management Agency (FEMA) launched the Building Resilient Infrastructure and Communities (BRIC) program to award predisaster mitigation grants, superseding the previous Pre-Disaster Mitigation Grant Program.

FEMA asked the Homeland Security Operational Analysis Center (HSOAC) to develop metrics—quantitative measurements of important concepts—that can inform decisionmaking for the BRIC Pre-Disaster Mitigation Grant Program. HSOAC engaged in a dialogue with FEMA leadership, examined key pieces of legislation, and reviewed stakeholder feedback submitted during a program design comment period to understand the measurement needs of the program. The research team established three primary lines of effort (LoEs) for this analysis, as shown in Table S.1, which also articulates each LoE's objective and the approach used in analysis.

Section 203 of the Stafford Act provides at least 21 directives for the BRIC program that metrics development could support. In some cases, these directives establish competing priorities. Section 203 does not specify a procedure for balancing these priorities, leaving it to the discretion of FEMA to design program policy that makes

Table S.1
Three Research Lines of Effort for Developing Building Resilient Infrastructure and Community Program Metrics

LoE Focus	LoE Objective	Research Approach
Indirect benefits	Measure how a mitigation project averts economic losses across the entire community	Conduct a document review of existing economic methods; blend techniques best suited for mitigation modeling
Applicant institutional capability (AIC)	Measure applicant capability to propose high-quality projects and execute them on time/on budget	Read analogous institutional capacity-relevant documents and interview subject-matter experts (SMEs) about experiences as/with applicants; develop an applicant capacity assessment scorecard
Community resilience	Measure community resilience—the ability of a community to prepare for, adapt to, and recover from disruption	Conduct a document review of existing resilience and vulnerability measures thought to be in use at FEMA; develop assessment scorecard of existing measures

reasonable trade-offs among them. This policy is likely to continue evolving over the next few years. We summarize these directives as five broad themes:

- The BRIC program must be effective and cost-effective.
- Disaster risk should inform allocation of funds.
- Applicant commitment to mitigation should inform allocation of funds.
- BRIC projects should be consistent with other mitigation initiatives.
- BRIC projects should benefit society.

Metrics would enable BRIC decisionmakers to monitor and improve compliance with these directives in two ways. First, they would inform grant application decisionmaking, both in terms of application merit and supporting applicants through the application process. Second, they would inform performance measurement in terms of estimation program effectiveness, program fairness, and implicit trade-offs being made among Section 203 directives. Mindful of the different use cases, varied priorities, and evolving program policy, we strove to develop versatile metrics that could be useful to BRIC decisionmakers in many ways.

Findings from the Three Lines of Effort

Indirect Benefits

Indirect consequences reflect the economic impacts on people and businesses who are connected to businesses and infrastructure that a disaster directly affects. When estimating the degree to which hazard mitigation projects are expected to benefit the broader community, it is imperative to account for indirect consequences because the economic impacts of a disaster may be predominantly indirect. The approach we used to determine suitable methods for projecting indirect benefits in the context of the BRIC program contained two phases. First, we reviewed the existing literature to identify methodologies appropriate for estimating the economic effects of natural disasters and mitigation projects; this review established input-output (I-O) models and computable general equilibrium (CGE) models as possible approaches. Second, we weighed the benefits and drawbacks to each approach against the backdrop provided by the BRIC program.

Our analysis informed a number of findings. However, all those findings start with a note of caution. Any model of indirect benefits must make aggressive assumptions. Recovery outcomes for natural disasters depend on many detailed nuances of the scenario—the natural hazard, terrain, built environment, structure, response, and so on—and all practical modeling options simplify these nuances to generic, conceptual representations of the event. Many of these nuances are currently either not knowable in advance or not cost-effective to model for each mitigation project. As such, mitigation benefit models can currently only project a broad approximation of the outcome.

That caveat aside, a notable advantage of the I-O approach is its practicality, which itself consists of a number of dimensions. First, I-O models are less technically complex than CGE models. Second, the approach generalizes in a way that makes it straightforward to apply consistently across state, local, tribal, and territorial governments. Third, the approach can rely on publicly available data. Fourth, the approach's relative simplicity requires users to have comparatively lower technical expertise. Moreover, the approach is well suited to estimating the impacts of shorter-term disaster disruptions. The I-O approach also contains drawbacks. I-O models are generally *static*, meaning that they do not capture time-varying changes in the economic environment or optimal behavioral responses to those changes. This results in a tendency to produce estimates closer to the upper bound of possible disaster impacts. Additionally, traditional I-O approaches only capture indirect effects arising from "backward" or "upstream" supply relationships and thus miss the "downstream" or "forward" indirect effects of a disaster. Finally, I-O models are less well suited to estimating the impacts of longer-term disaster disruptions.

The alternative to I-O models—CGE models—can also be fully calibrated using publicly available data and contain certain advantages over I-O models. Their ability to capture price effects and optimal firm and consumer responses make them more suitable for estimating the effects of longer-term disruptions. However, this capability makes these models less desirable for estimating the impacts of short-term disruptions, when price changes and optimizing behavior may not be possible or realistic. Assuming optimizing behavior also results in the models having a tendency to produce estimates closer to the lower bound of possible impacts. CGE models can also leverage social accounting matrices data to provide more disaggregated estimates than traditional I-O approaches; however, doing so comes at the cost of practicality and ease of use. While CGE models are more complex than I-O models, both models ultimately rest on similar underlying infrastructure; there is substantial overlap in data structure, model inputs, and model outputs. Each type of model could also be integrated into Hazus as a relatively automated component and could leverage Hazus's existing capabilities to calibrate some key model inputs.[1]

Applicant Institutional Capability

This LoE researched how AIC—the set of assets and capabilities that enables applicants to effectively propose and manage mitigation grants—might affect the savings to the Disaster Relief Fund (DRF) that hazard mitigation projects are expected to provide. A number of AIC factors affect project performance, such as prior experience with hazard mitigation grants, size and capacity of FEMA's state hazard mitigation officers, and access to technical expertise. When all other circumstances are similar, reduced AIC might result either in increased costs to complete the project or in decreased expected benefits from the project. Both increased costs and decreased expected benefits diminish the project's expected benefit/cost ratio.

We drew insights from the relevant institutional capacity documents on AIC to inform an interview protocol conducted with 11 FEMA SMEs and developed an AIC assessment scorecard. Our synthesis of the interview responses underscored that the most important internal factors for high-performing applicants were an appropriately trained and skilled workforce, prior experience, and access to management and technical capabilities. The specific assessment criteria derived from this synthesis include general and key staff turnover, staff skill/expertise and prior experience with predisaster mitigation projects and grants, management/administration capabilities, and access to technical expertise to propose predisaster mitigation projects. The identification of these criteria informed our finding that evaluations of applicant capability should focus on staff retention, staff skill and experience, management capability, and technical capability.

In addition to internal factors, FEMA SMEs in our interviews also mentioned external factors outside an applicant's control that influence project performance—such as disaster disruption and weather delays. FEMA SMEs offered additional suggestions for improvement, including a better understanding of risks, adoption of disaster resistance codes, transparent grant award processes, incentives, FEMA partnerships, and using existing measures, like the Community Rating System (CRS) and Building Code Effectiveness Grading Schedule (BCEGS), as capacity indicators.

---

[1] Hazus is FEMA's computerized methodology for estimating potential direct losses from disasters. It processes information on the geographic distribution of disaster risks and fixed assets, using this information to estimate the direct physical, economic, and social impacts of disasters. For further information, see FEMA, 2020b.

Community Resilience

The third LoE focused on community resilience. According to the National Institute of Standards and Technology (NIST) definition, "community resilience is the ability to prepare for anticipated hazards, adapt to changing conditions, and withstand and recovery rapidly from disruptions."[2] Using this definition, we conducted a review of community resilience measures thought to be in use at FEMA, profiling ten measures of resilience, vulnerability, and/or building code quality. We then created an evaluation assessment scorecard that FEMA SMEs can use to determine what community resilience measures are best suited to support the needs of the BRIC program, focusing on four factors: (1) ability to measure key aspects of the NIST community resilience concept; (2) ability to measure Stafford Act compliance with related concepts; (3) practicality, including scientific validations work conducted to date; and (4) ability to meet BRIC-specific needs for a hazard-neutral measure that BRIC grants can plausibly affect.

Two HSOAC SMEs conducted a test run of the evaluation framework on the ten measures, finding that the framework was both useful and capable of providing insight. While we provide no recommendations for a specific measure, we do note three general insights from the evaluation exercise. First, measures that focus on actions that communities can take may be more useful to BRIC than measures that focus on difficult-to-change census population characteristics. CRS in FEMA's National Flood Insurance Program is an example of an action-based measure. Second, vulnerability measures based on difficult-to-change census population characteristics may be better suited to measuring equity gaps in program outcomes, especially if they can easily be decomposed into component measures to provide more detailed insights. The Centers for Disease Control and Prevention's Social Vulnerability Index is an example of a census-based vulnerability measure that can be easily decomposed into straightforward components. Third, building codes are heavily emphasized in the revised Stafford Act Section 203 but are often missing from resilience measures—especially census-based measures. Most options for measuring resilience may need to be augmented with a building code adoption/enforcement measure to improve statutory compliance. The Insurance Services Office's BCEGS is an example of a building code adoption and enforcement quality measure.

Recommendations

We provide 11 recommendations based on the findings of the three LoEs, along with one overarching recommendation. Chapter Six provides more detail on each recommendation, including the rationale for it. Here, we summarize them in Table S.2.

---

2 National Institute of Standards and Technology, *Community Resilience | NIST*, June 18, 2020.

Table S.2
Recommendations

Overarching recommendation	1. Develop a strategy for addressing known DRF cost drivers
Indirect benefits recommendations	2. In the near term, use a tailored I-O model to measure communitywide indirect benefits of mitigation projects
	3. Integrate the indirect benefits model into Hazus and automate as much as possible
	4. Decide whether a CGE model or I-O model best suits the long-term needs of BRIC
AIC recommendations	5. Evaluate applicant capability to propose/execute high-quality mitigation projects and develop strategies for supporting lower-capability applicants
	6. In evaluating applicant capability, focus on staff retention, staff skills and experience, management capacity, and technical capacity
Community resilience recommendations	7. Periodically assess community resilience measures and encourage usage at FEMA of measures that performed well on the assessment
	8. In evaluating community resilience, focus on resilience, Stafford Act compliance, scientific validation, and practicality
	9. Use action-based community resilience metrics to evaluate performance
	10. Consider population-based community resilience metrics to evaluate equity gaps
	11. Consider building code adoption/enforcement metrics to improve statutory compliance if not already part of the community resilience metric chosen

Acknowledgments

We appreciate and acknowledge the many people who contributed to the completion of this report. We offer our thanks to the reviewers of this study—Anu Narayanan, Benjamin Preston, Costa Samaras, and Aaron Strong—for providing insightful feedback on this report and to the Federal Emergency Management Agency interviewees who shared their perspectives and experiences with us. We also gratefully acknowledge Emma Westerman, Kristen Hatcher, and the Building Resilient Infrastructure and Communities program's leadership at the Federal Emergency Management Agency for providing support, guidance, and insight throughout the project.

Abbreviations

BCEGS	Building Code Effectiveness Grading Schedule
BEA	Bureau of Economic Analysis
BRIC	Building Resilient Infrastructure and Communities
CDBG	Community Development Block Grant
CDC	Centers for Disease Control and Prevention
CDRI	Community Disaster Resilience Index
CES	constant elasticity of substitution
CGE	computable general equilibrium
CRIA	Community Resilience Indicator Analysis
CRS	Community Rating System
DOTMLPF+R/G/S	Doctrine, Organization, Training, Materiel, Leadership, Personnel, Facilities plus Regulations, Grants, and Standards framework
DRF	Disaster Relief Fund
DRRA	Disaster Recovery Reform Act of 2018
EPA	Environment Protection Agency
FEMA	Federal Emergency Management Agency
HICD	Human and Institutional Capacity Development model
HSOAC	Homeland Security Operational Analysis Center
IA	individual assistance
IBHS	Institute of Building and Home Safety
IMPLAN	Impact Analysis for Planning
I-O	input-output models
ISO	Insurance Services Office
LoE	line of effort
MSA	metropolitan statistical area

NAICS	North American Industry Classification System
NFIP	National Flood Insurance Program
NIST	National Institute of Standards and Technology
PA	public assistance
PBWW	Portland Bureau of Water Works
PDM	Pre-Disaster Mitigation Grant Program
RCI	Resilience Capacity Index
RIMS II	Regional Input-Output Modeling System
SAM	social accounting matrices
SLTT	state, local, tribal, and territorial
SME	subject-matter expert
SoVI	Social Vulnerability Index
SVI	Social Vulnerability Index
UNCDF	United Nations Capital Development Fund
UNDP	United Nations Development Programme
USAID	U.S. Agency for International Development

CHAPTER ONE

Introduction

Background

The Robert T. Stafford Disaster Relief and Emergency Assistance Act (henceforth, the "Stafford Act") provides the key legal foundation for federal disaster response and recovery assistance activities. Recognizing that prevention can be more effective than response, Section 203 of the Stafford Act authorizes establishing a program to provide assistance to state and local governments to take predisaster mitigation measures. It requires that such measures be "cost-effective and designed to reduce injuries, loss of life, and damage and destruction of property, including damage to critical services and facilities under the jurisdiction of the States or local governments."[1] Acting on the Stafford Act's authority, the Federal Emergency Management Agency (FEMA) provides grant funding to state, local, tribal, and territorial (SLTT) governments to carry out mitigation projects. The funding is primarily allocated through a competitive application process, with some stipulations to ensure that at least a minimum level of funding goes to each state and territory.[2]

Section 1234 of the Disaster Recovery Reform Act of 2019 (DRRA) amends Section 203 of the Stafford Act. It emphasizes the importance of public infrastructure, building codes, cost-effectiveness, resilience, and the targeting of places where disaster declarations have occurred in the last seven years. It also adjusts the way that the program is funded, such that it now receives an amount of up to 6 percent of certain disaster response/recovery spending estimates for each disaster.

In response, FEMA launched the Building Resilient Infrastructure and Community (BRIC) program to award predisaster mitigation grants, superseding the previous Pre-Disaster Mitigation Grant Program (PDM). FEMA convened working groups to design the new program, which developed six guiding principles:

- BRIC should build capacity and capability in communities. This can be viewed as a strategy for improving community resilience.

---

1 U.S. Code, Title 42, Section 5133, Predisaster Hazard Mitigation, January 3, 2012.

2 Includes the District of Columbia.

- BRIC should encourage and enable innovation.
- Related to principle two, BRIC should maintain flexibility in terms of what kinds of projects it funds. These two guidelines can be viewed as a strong recognition that innovative ideas and precisely targeted mitigation solutions are better suited than one-size-fits-all generic molds.
- BRIC should enable large projects. This guideline can be viewed as crucial for emphasizing infrastructure, because the cost of such projects can be quite large relative to the amount of funding the program receives in years without major disasters.
- BRIC should provide consistency. This guideline can be viewed as important for counterbalancing the variable nature of its funding stream. BRIC is funded with a percentage of disaster response/recovery assistance; adjusted for inflation, annual individual assistance (IA) and public assistance (PA) has varied from $1.4 billion to $12.6 billion in the last decade.
- BRIC should encourage public-private partnerships, mobilizing the full resources of the community to mitigating the negative consequences of future disasters.

Objectives and Approach

FEMA asked the Homeland Security Operational Analysis Center (HSOAC) to develop metrics—quantitative measurements of important concepts—that can inform decisionmaking for the BRIC Pre-Disaster Mitigation Grant Program. HSOAC engaged in a dialogue with FEMA leadership, examined key pieces of legislature, and reviewed stakeholder feedback submitted during a program design comment period to understand the measurement needs of the program. Three primary lines of effort (LoEs) were established, which are described in Table 1.1.

Midway through the project, we had a conversation with FEMA leadership and the Office of Management and Budget about additional analysis needed to support the new program. At that time, we added a fourth LoE to conduct an analysis on FEMA's benefit-cost analysis tool, which is the primary tool used to estimate project cost-effectiveness. Because this fourth LoE was a late addition, the results of that analysis will be documented as a separate briefing and are not discussed further in this report.

During the metrics development process, FEMA discussed two potential uses for metrics—grant application decisionmaking and performance evaluation. Application decisionmaking includes both evaluation of merit and evaluation of applicant need for support. Performance evaluation includes both evaluation of outcomes and evaluation of program fairness.

Behind these use cases lies the Stafford Act, the primary authorizing legislation for FEMA. As itemized in Table 2.1 in Chapter Two, Section 203 specifies at least

Table 1.1
Three Research Lines of Effort for Developing Building Resilient Infrastructure and Community Program Metrics

LoE Focus	LoE Objective	LoE Approach
Indirect benefits	Measure how a mitigation project averts economic losses across the entire community	Conduct a document review of existing economic methods; blend techniques best suited for mitigation modeling
Applicant institutional capability (AIC)	Measure applicant capability to propose high-quality projects and execute them on time/on budget	Read analogous institutional capacity-relevant documents and interview subject-matter experts (SMEs) about experiences as/with applicants; develop an applicant capacity assessment scorecard
Community resilience	Develop an assessment framework for evaluating community resilience metrics—the ability of a community to prepare for, adapt to, and recover from disruption	Conduct a document review of existing resilience and vulnerability measures thought to be in use at FEMA; develop assessment scorecard of existing measures

21 directives for the BRIC program that are relevant for application decisionmaking and/or performance evaluation. Many of these directives establish competing priorities, leaving FEMA to determine how to balance them and ensure compliance. Metric-informed grant decisionmaking rules and performance-evaluation monitoring provide options for ensuring compliance at the individual project and programwide impact levels, respectively. They also provide decisionmakers with visibility on the implicit trade-offs they are making among competing priorities. Mindful of the different use cases, varied priorities, and evolving program policy, we strove to develop versatile metrics that could be useful to BRIC decisionmakers in many ways.

Scope

Viewing the three LoEs as a consistent whole, we developed tools for assessing future projects based on information that can generally be gathered during the application process rather than by focusing on the analysis of historical data. There are three reasons for this. First, the time scale of occurrence for most severe disasters is much longer than the entire history of the Pre-Disaster Mitigation Grant Program, so it is difficult to truly evaluate historical performance. For example, since 1906, the conterminous United States has had only two earthquakes that exceeded 7.5 on the Richter scale.[3] This suggests that the conterminous United States might reasonably expect to see an earthquake exceed 7.5 only about every 57 years on average—a time scale that is longer than the entire life span of FEMA. Second, given long time scales of occurrence, con-

[3] U.S. Geological Survey, "Earthquake Hazards," webpage, undated.

ditions are likely to be substantially different in the future than they were in the past because of technical change, evolving land use, and climate change impacts like sea-level rise. Third, evaluating the effectiveness of mitigation is difficult to do solely based on historical data because it always involves comparing the events that happened to the events that *would have* happened if the mitigation measure had or had not been in place. Disasters, built structures, and communities are not uniform, and this diversity makes comparative analysis difficult to do across communities.

However, as a matter of due diligence, we did examine historical expenditures to understand what has driven past costs to the Disaster Relief Fund (DRF) and what lessons that might have for designing a cost-effective mitigation grant program. This analysis is detailed in Appendix A. Based on the analysis, we note the following:

- Historical DRF disaster response/recovery costs have been driven by outlier events. During the 2004–2019 period, 19 disaster declarations associated with Hurricanes Katrina, Sandy, and Maria accounted for more PA and IA assistance costs than the other 1,955 declarations we examined.
- Even excluding Katrina, Sandy, and Maria, most costs appear to be driven by small segments of declarations. Looking at costs attributable to specific metropolitan areas, the Houston and Miami metropolitan statistical areas (MSAs) account for 20 percent of all PA/IA costs. Looking at costs in metro and non-metro areas combined, 63 percent of costs were attributable to hurricanes and severe storms that damaged roads, bridges, public buildings, and public utilities[4] and/or affected low-elevation cities near the stretch of coast between Galveston, Texas, and Miami, Florida.

Given the previous scope caveats, we did not pursue this further in developing our metrics. However, we do feel that this is an important policy consideration for BRIC program decisionmakers.

Organization of This Document

In the remainder of this report, we first discuss in more detail the BRIC program legal authorities laid out above and their connections to the LoEs (Chapter Two). We discuss the three LoEs that were the focus of this study in Chapters Three, Four, and Five, focusing on the approaches taken for each LoE and what we found. Chapter Six offers some conclusions and recommendations.

The report has a number of appendixes. Appendix A examines the historical costs of providing assistance after a declared disaster, drawing out some of the impli-

4 In terms of FEMA PA project categories, these are Category C (roads and bridges), Category E (public buildings), and Category F (public utilities).

cations for mitigation program policy. Appendix B contains more detail on the indirect benefits effort shown in Chapter Three. Appendix C provides a discussion of the international development literature that is summarized in Chapter Four on AIC. The full discussion of the literature identified abundant scholarly research and practitioner-oriented guidance on institutional capacity—both what constitutes it and how to bolster it. This review helped to inform the development of the semistructured interview protocol (Appendix D) used in the analysis. Appendix E provides the analysis codebook for the AIC effort.

CHAPTER TWO

Supporting Compliance: Relationship Between Lines of Effort and the Building Resilient Infrastructure and Community Program's Statutory Requirements

As discussed above, the BRIC program was authorized by the DRRA of 2018, which was signed into law on October 5, 2018, as part of the FAA Reauthorization Act of 2018.[1] The DRRA made a series of reforms to the Stafford Act, the hallmark federal legislation providing FEMA with many of its legal authorities for disaster response, recovery, and mitigation programs and activities.[2] Section 1234 (National Public Infrastructure Pre-Disaster Hazard Mitigation) of the DRRA modified and built on FEMA's existing PDM to create a new program for federal predisaster mitigation assistance. FEMA named this program BRIC.[3] The BRIC program provides predisaster hazard mitigation grants to eligible SLTT applicants. It is funded through a new DRF set-aside that may provide greater reliability and predictability for federal predisaster mitigation projects.

This chapter describes BRIC's major statutory requirements, including its goals and objectives, program structure, applicant evaluation criteria, and funding mechanism. It then explains how the LoEs in this report relate to BRIC's legal authorities and responsibilities.

The Building Resilient Infrastructure and Community Program's Major Statutory Requirements

Under the statutory language authorizing BRIC, the President may establish a program providing technical and financial assistance to eligible SLTTs for predisaster

[1] Public Law 115-254, FAA Reauthorization Act of 2018, October 5, 2018.

[2] Public Law 100-707, Robert T. Stafford Disaster Relief and Emergency Assistance Act, November 23, 1988.

[3] FEMA, "Webinar Series 2019: Building Resilient Infrastructure and Communities," webpage, last updated August 22, 2019b.

hazard mitigation measures.[4] To be eligible for BRIC funding, hazard mitigation projects must be "cost-effective" and "designed to reduce injuries, loss of life, and damage and destruction of property, including damage to critical services and facilities under the jurisdiction of the States or local government."[5] The law also states that SLTT applicants must demonstrate "the ability to form effective public-private natural disaster hazard mitigation partnerships" before receiving BRIC awards.[6]

The Stafford Act already specified that technical and financial assistance could be used to support effective public-private partnerships, "improve the assessment of a community's vulnerability to natural hazards" and "establish hazard mitigation priorities." The amended text adds that technical and financial assistance may be used to enforce building codes and "implement the latest published editions of relevant consensus-based codes, specifications, and standards that incorporate the latest hazard-resistant designs," as well as establish minimum acceptable criteria for residential structures.[7]

In addition to the requirements above, the amended Stafford Act puts forward 12 statutory criteria[8] for award determinations. The program must "take into account" these criteria in selecting potential recipients[9] and in awarding assistance.[10] However, no hierarchy or prioritization is specified, so it is left to the program to determine how to make trade-offs when criteria conflict. The 12 criteria (paraphrased here) specify that the program should take into account

- the type and severity of the hazard
- SLTT commitment to reducing damages from future natural disasters
- SLTT commitment to support nonfederal contributions to hazard mitigation projects
- project contribution to state mitigation priorities
- project consistency with other assistance provided under the Stafford Act
- project cost-effectiveness and whether it has identified meaningful/definable outcomes
- if the SLTT has submitted a hazard mitigation plan, the project's consistency with the plan
- opportunities to maximize net benefits to society

4 42 U.S.C. 5133(b).

5 42 U.S.C. 5133(b).

6 42 U.S.C. 5133(b).

7 42 U.S.C. 5133(e).

8 42 U.S.C. 5133(g).

9 42 U.S.C. 5133(d).

10 42 U.S.C. 5133(f).

- whether the project funds activities in small impoverished communities
- SLTT commitment to facilitating the adoption and enforcement of hazard-resistant building standards
- project potential to increase community resilience
- "other criteria as the President establishes in consultation" with SLTT governments.

Section 1234 of the DRRA added two of the 12 evaluation criteria. FEMA decisionmakers must now take into consideration two things: (1) the extent to which an SLTT facilitates adoption/enforcement of consensus-based codes and standards, including hazard-resistant designs and minimum standards for design/construction/maintenance of structures that may be eligible for disaster assistance, and (2) whether the project funds activities that increase resilience. Resilience is not defined in either Section 1234 of the DRRA or the Stafford Act.

DRRA Section 1234 and the Stafford Act also establish the BRIC program funding structure and other program requirements. BRIC is funded by a 6-percent set-aside from the DRF, excluding the DRF base. The 6-percent DRF set-aside will be drawn from the estimated aggregate grant amounts for seven specific Stafford Act programs administered by FEMA but does not reduce funding otherwise available to them. These programs are

- Essential Assistance (Section 403)
- Repair, Restoration, and Replacement of Damaged Facilities (Section 406)
- Debris Removal (Section 407)
- Federal Assistance to Individuals and Households (Section 408)
- Unemployment Assistance (Section 410)
- Crisis Counseling Assistance and Training (Section 416)
- Public Assistance Program Alternative Procedures (Section 428).[11]

The DRRA also adds language on use of funding under Stafford Act Sections 203 and 404 for wildfires, windstorms, and earthquakes. DRRA Section 1204 states that Section 404 hazard mitigation assistance can be used for wildfires, even without a major disaster declaration. Section 1205 permits use of Hazard Mitigation Grant Program and PDM funding for wildfire and windstorm mitigation and provides examples of permissible activities. Finally, Section 1233 permits Hazard Mitigation Grant Program and PDM assistance for earthquakes.[12]

---

[11] 42 U.S.C. 5133(i).

[12] FAA Reauthorization Act of 2018.

How the Homeland Security Operational Analysis Center's Lines of Effort Relate to the Building Resilient Infrastructure and Community Program's Legal Authorities and Responsibilities

As an organizational convenience to facilitate our work, we grouped the Stafford Act, Section 203 requirements, and related guidance into five rough "themes" and used them to inform the progress of our LoEs. Table 2.1 presents these themes.

Our metrics quantify concepts that are most directly related to the cost-effectiveness and societal benefit themes. The **indirect benefits LoE** provides insight on cost-effectiveness because it quantifies how a project averts economic disruption across a community. This provides a way of measuring the broader economic benefits of a project, which can be compared with its projected costs. In providing tools for modeling disruption and recovery from disruption, the same metric also quantifies economic resilience and could be used to pick projects that will enhance it. In addition, this LoE provides insight on societal benefit because it is a measure of the economic importance of a given asset. Projects that improve economically important assets may provide societal benefit even in the absence of a natural disaster.

The **AIC LoE** provides insight on cost-effectiveness because it identifies risk factors that may make it difficult for applicants to identify opportunities for highly effective projects and to execute those projects on time and on budget. AIC also contributes to societal benefit in that it identifies disadvantaged applicants, potentially enabling the program to provide enhanced support for them.

The **community resilience LoE** provides insight on effectiveness because it identifies measures that can be used to measure improvement in community resilience and prioritize projects that can improve community resilience. It also identifies measures that can be used to identify vulnerable communities. This may also contribute to societal benefit in that it potentially enables the program to provide enhanced support for disadvantaged communities or prioritize projects that will have the side benefit of improving general quality of life in those communities. In addition, this LoE also notes which measures provide some visibility on commitment to mitigation, in terms of building code adoption and enforcement.

These LoEs do not generally provide insight on risk or unity of effort. Unity of effort does not require significant metrics development work because it can easily be addressed within the existing application process. Incorporating disaster risk into BRIC decisionmaking is a particularly challenging problem that requires substantial resources, so we have mobilized a separate HSOAC team to potentially address it as part of a separate project. However, Appendix A provides an analysis of past DRF IA/PA cost drivers, which is a first step toward understanding future cost risks.

Table 2.1
Five "Themes" Among the Program Requirements in Stafford Act, Section 203

Theme	Requirement
Effectiveness/cost-effectiveness: project will make a measurable difference, diminishing losses, increasing resilience, and lowering DRF costs	• Cost-effective (b, e) • Designed to reduce injuries, loss of life, and damage and destruction of property, including damage to critical SLTT services and facilities (b) • Project is cost-effective with meaningful/clearly defined outcomes (f) • Project increases resilience (f)
Risk: applicant works to identify hazard risks and projects are crafted to address those risks	• SLTT has identified natural disaster hazards within its jurisdiction (c) • Funds may be used to improve assessment of community hazard risks (e) • SLTT is within a state that has received a disaster declaration in the last seven years (f) • Project takes into account type and severity of hazard (f) • Funds may be used for mitigation planning and developing priorities (e)
Commitment to mitigation: applicant actively works to mitigate hazards and encourage mitigation	• SLTT has demonstrated the ability to form effective public-private mitigation partnerships (c) • Funds may be used to support public-private partnerships (e) • SLTT commitment to reduce future disaster damage (f) • SLTT commitment to support nonfederal hazard mitigation (f) • SLTT facilitates adoption/enforcement of hazard-resistant building standards for the purpose of protecting health, safety, and welfare of buildings' users from disasters (f) • Funds may be used to establish and enforce hazard-resistant building standards (e) • Up to 10 percent of funds may be used to disseminate information on cost-effective mitigation (e)
Unity of effort: applicant strives for unity of effort with federal, state, and private-sector mitigation initiatives	• Project contributes to state mitigation goals/priorities (f) • Project is consistent with other Stafford-funded initiatives (f) • Project is consistent with SLTT mitigation plan (f)
Societal benefit: project benefits society, including disadvantaged communities	• Project maximizes net benefits to society (f) • Some projects funded in small impoverished community (f)

NOTE: The letters in parentheses indicate subsections of Section 203 of the Stafford Act.

CHAPTER THREE

Indirect Benefits Line of Effort

Introduction

Consistent with the *DHS Risk Lexicon*, we break the total economic effects of a natural disaster into two conceptual parts: direct consequences and indirect consequences.[1] Direct consequences (either benefits or costs) capture economic impacts that are directly associated with the natural disaster itself. For example, a flood may damage a manufacturing plant, thus causing production rates to decrease. The value of this lost output would be considered a direct economic consequence of the flood. Other examples of direct economic consequences include damage to buildings and lifeline infrastructure. FEMA estimates direct benefits using the Benefit Cost Toolkit. This Excel-based tool analyzes information on the features of a structure, occupancy/uses of the structure, hazard risks at that location, and proposed mitigation measures. Based on that information, it estimates how much damage the structure is likely to incur during its useful lifetime, both with and without the mitigation measure, including property damage, loss of income, and injury/death on the premises. For select public services, the tool also involves continuity of service in the benefits, where the value of those services is equal to the taxpayer costs of providing them. The benefit of the mitigation project is calculated as the difference between the monetary value of the losses that the structure would incur if the mitigation measure was not in place and the value of the losses it would incur if the mitigation measure was in place. To be eligible for grant funding, the tool must find that the benefit of the mitigation project is equal to or greater than the cost of funding it.[2]

Unlike direct consequences, indirect consequences reflect the economic impacts on those businesses that are connected to directly affected businesses and lifeline infrastructure. These could be either benefits or costs. An example would be the consequences on firms that use goods produced by the aforementioned manufacturing plant in their own production processes that no longer have access to the same level of supply

1 Risk Steering Committee, *DHS Risk Lexicon*, Washington, D.C.: U.S. Department of Homeland Security, 2010.

2 FEMA, "Benefit-Cost Analysis," webpage, last updated February 14, 2020a.

as they did prior to the flood. The projected economic benefits of predisaster mitigation efforts arise from a counterfactual comparison. They represent the expected difference in the economic effects of a natural disaster across two scenarios: one in which disaster mitigation activities take place prior to the disaster and one in which they do not.

This chapter focuses on methods to compute the indirect economic benefits of predisaster mitigation activities. Methods for estimating direct and indirect consequences differ, although they are often related because indirect consequences are a function of direct consequences, as in our example. When quantifying how much hazard mitigation projects are expected to benefit the broader community, one must account for both direct and indirect consequences because the economic impacts of a disaster may be largely indirect. The rest of this chapter proceeds as follows. First, we describe the approach we used to identify suitable ways for estimating the indirect benefits of mitigation projects for the BRIC program. This involved an extensive survey of existing methods and capabilities, with emphasis placed on dimensions particularly important in the BRIC context. Second, we report the findings of our analysis in two parts. In the first part, we describe two identified candidate approaches for estimating indirect benefits: input-output (I-O) models and computable general equilibrium (CGE) models. In the second part of the findings, we discuss the benefits and drawbacks associated with each approach. Last, we conclude with a summary of the material contained in the chapter.

Methods

Our approach to determining appropriate methods for estimating the indirect economic benefits of disaster mitigation projects consisted of two phases. First, we surveyed the existing literature to identify methods that either have been used or could be used to estimate the economic effects of natural disasters and disaster mitigation efforts. This phase of the analysis identified I-O and CGE models as candidate methods for the BRIC program. Second, we examined the benefits and drawbacks to each approach in the context of applying them to the BRIC program. In this stage, we devoted particular attention to the following: (1) the breadth of disaster and disaster mitigation scenarios each method could be applied to and the accuracy of each method across different types of scenarios; (2) the practicality of each method across different timelines for operationalization; and (3) the ability of each method to leverage existing capabilities (e.g., those contained in FEMA's Hazus tool).[3] The findings derived

[3] Hazus is FEMA's computerized methodology for estimating potential direct losses from disasters. It processes information on the geographic distribution of disaster risks and fixed assets, using this information to estimate the direct physical, economic, and social impacts of disasters. For further information, see FEMA, 2020b.

from our approach are reported in the following section. Appendix B contains a more detailed discussion of the methodologies.

Findings—Two Strategies for Modeling Indirect Benefits

We identified I-O and CGE as the two most widely accepted modeling strategies for estimating the economic benefits of hazard mitigation. However, all modeling options in this area of research come with a significant caveat. Any model of indirect benefits must make aggressive assumptions. Recovery outcomes for natural disasters depend on many detailed nuances of the scenario—the natural hazard, terrain, built environment, structure, response, and so on—and all practical modeling options simplify these nuances to a generic, conceptual representation of the event. Many of these nuances are currently either not knowable in advance or not cost-effective to model for each mitigation project. As such, mitigation benefit models can currently only project a broad approximation of the outcome.

Input-Output Models

I-O models quantify the connectedness among sectors in a national or regional economy. More specifically, they capture the degree to which the goods and services (outputs) produced by each sector serve as inputs to the production processes of other sectors. The canonical model is attributed to Wassily Leontief; since then, its formulation has been extended in a number of ways and used by policymakers in a wide variety of contexts.[4] A core feature of I-O models is their ability to trace how a change in the output of a given sector affects all the sectors providing production inputs to that sector and all the sectors providing inputs to those sectors and so on; I-O models ultimately allow one to estimate the effects of an initial industry-level change on the entire economy. This feature of I-O models makes them particularly attractive for quantifying the economic effects of natural disasters, especially because the models are supported

[4] See, for example, Wassily W. Leontief, "Input-Output Economics," *Scientific American*, Vol. 185, No. 4, 1951a; Wassily W. Leontief, *The Structure of the American Economy*, 1919–1939, 2nd ed., New York: Oxford University Press, 1951b; Wassily W. Leontief, *Input-Output Economics*, New York: Oxford University Press, 1966; Yacov Y. Haimes, Barry M. Horowitz, James H. Lambert, Joost R. Santos, Chenyang Lian, and Kenneth G. Crowther, "Inoperability Input-Output Model for Interdependent Infrastructure Sectors. I: Theory and Methodology," *Journal of Infrastructure Systems*, Vol. 11, No. 2, 2005a; Yacov Y. Haimes, Barry M. Horowitz, James H. Lambert, Joost R. Santos, Chenyang Lian, and Kenneth G. Crowther, "Inoperability Input-Output Model for Interdependent Infrastructure Sectors. II: Case Studies," *Journal of Infrastructure Systems*, Vol. 11, No. 2, 2005b; Chenyang Lian and Yacov Y. Haimes, "Managing the Risk of Terrorism to Interdependent Infrastructure Systems Through the Dynamic Inoperability Input-Output Model," *Systems Engineering*, Vol. 9, No. 3, 2006; Ronald E. Miller and Peter D. Blair, *Input-Output Analysis: Foundations and Extensions*, 2nd ed., New York: Cambridge University Press, 2009; and Yasuhide Okuyama and Joost R. Santos, "Disaster Impact and Input–Output Analysis," *Economic Systems Research*, Vol. 26, No. 1, 2014.

by public data-collection efforts. The methodology also provides a way to estimate the economic benefits of predisaster mitigation activities. Mitigation efforts dampen the initial disruption caused by a disaster, which then results in relatively lower indirect economic impacts compared to a counterfactual scenario where no mitigation measures took place.

All economic activity in the United States over a given period can be partitioned among all the sectors (industries) that compose it; different (though related) sector classification schemes exist that define what these sectors are. Perhaps the two most prominent classification systems are the North American Industry Classification System (NAICS) and the Standard Industrial Classification system, which each provide a hierarchical categorization of economic sectors. That is, each contains an aggregated list of sectors that make up the economy—for example, mining and manufacturing—that may be expanded into more disaggregated lists, where sectors such as mining and manufacturing are broken down into increasingly more specific subcategories like coal mining and beverage manufacturing.

When considering the indirect economic effects of a natural disaster, one needs to disaggregate industries at the regional level to capture the unique characteristics of the regional economy hit by the disaster. For instance, different regions have different industrial makeups where one region might be dominated by agriculture and another region by industrial manufacturing. Thus, disasters will affect different regions uniquely; as a result, the composition of the I-O table must reflect these unique economic characteristics to avoid estimation errors. Aggregation errors will always be present given the finite limit of the number of industrial accounts in the matrix; however, the more disaggregated the I-O table, the higher the ability to reduce aggregation errors.[5] Disaggregation of the sectors does present issues in itself where the complex interconnectedness of the region with its surrounding neighbors can be challenging to capture.[6] For instance, the ability for I-O tables to capture interregional and international trade is limited. Economic trade is an important component of any regional economy, and failure to capture trade can lead to estimation errors.[7]

Within a given sector, the economic value of the output it produces can be divided into the value of its output that is used in production by other sectors—known as intermediate goods and services—and the value of its output that is consumed "as is" by end users, such as households, businesses, and the government. The latter category is referred to as final goods and services; it consists of items that are not used to produce other items. The idea behind I-O models is to leverage data on intersector supply relationships to predict how a change in the final output of one or more sectors affects the

[5] J. M. Albala-Bertrand, *Disasters and the Networked Economy*, Oxon, UK: Routledge, 2014.

[6] Albala-Bertrand, 2014.

[7] Cletus Coughlin and Thomas B. Mandelbaum, "Social Vulnerability to Environmental Hazards," *Social Science Quarterly*, Vol. 84, No. 2, 2003; Albala-Bertrand, 2014.

value of total sectoral output for each sector in the economy, given the extent of intersectoral relationships observed in the data.

They accomplish this by constructing what are known as the **technical coefficients** and **total requirements** matrices. A technical coefficient describes the dollar value of inputs required of one sector by another to produce one dollar's worth of output. The coefficients embedded in the total requirements matrix represent, for each industry, the value of total inputs required to produce one dollar of final goods and services. These matrices serve to calibrate the expected effect of a change in the final output of a given sector on each sector that supplies it, either directly or indirectly, with production inputs.

The multipliers embedded in the total requirements matrix are referred to as Type I multipliers, which reflect only the indirect economic effects on industries. By incorporating data on payments to labor and capital, Type II multipliers can be constructed; Type II multipliers additionally capture projected effects on income, which subsequently affect demand for final goods and services. The use of data on payments to labor and capital also allows Type I multipliers to be calculated in terms of value added instead of output. Output-based I-O multipliers will double count some economic effects because the value of intermediate goods and services is also reflected in the prices of the final goods and services they were used to produce. Value-added multipliers avoid double counting by only estimating the effects on value added at each stage of the production process. The U.S. Bureau of Economic Analysis (BEA) publishes publicly available data on payments to labor and capital. These data are also contained in social accounting matrices (SAMs), which are a more granular form of I-O data that can, for example, be used to parse the projected economic effects on different socioeconomic groups.

As previously discussed, one needs to disaggregate the industrial accounts of an I-O table to reduce aggregation error. However, developing a disaggregated regional I-O table is not trivial; it requires both time- and labor-intensive data-collection methods.[8] This is why resources such as the BEA can make I-O analyses more accessible to state and local governments that wish to calculate the indirect economic effects of a disaster. However, developing a regional I-O table or using BEA resources present temporal limitations where data are either out of date from time-intensive collection periods or because the BEA data are only updated every five years or so. If the economic structure of the study region changes in the time between data collection and analysis, there could be estimation errors. Economies often change because of technol-

[8] Coughlin and Mandelbaum, 1991.

ogy, new inventions or methods of production, industrial expansion, or price changes. As a result, such temporal factors can limit the accuracy of I-O analyses.[9]

I-O models estimate the economic effects of a disaster through a "before-and-after" comparison; they take the expected change in final industry output following a disaster as an input and use the matrices described above to project how the initial, direct effect of the disaster ripples through the broader economy. The difference between the estimated total and direct economic effects constitutes the projected indirect economic effects. I-O models quantify the economic benefits of predisaster mitigation efforts by using the same type of estimation strategy we have just described. Conceptually, the projected economic benefits of predisaster mitigation activities are the expected difference between the value of lost economic output resulting from a natural disaster scenario when no such mitigation activities took place beforehand and the value of lost economic output resulting from the same disaster scenario when these activities had taken place beforehand. The difference between these two numbers represents the projected total economic value of the mitigation efforts—the value of sectoral output that would have been lost if the mitigation efforts had not been undertaken. Once again, taking the difference between the estimated total and direct economic effects results in the projected indirect economic effects.

The previously discussed limitations of aggregation constraints, spatial constraints, and temporal delays in data create uncertainty in the estimates.[10] Additionally, there are computational constraints on how the errors interact during the calculations that take place when the model is solved where the errors can create bias in the estimates.[11] It is therefore important for the analyst to be aware of these constraints when modeling regional economic impacts of natural disasters to estimate the indirect benefits. Maintaining awareness of the uncertainties coupled with the analyst's expertise on the region, the data, and the model can help minimize estimation errors and manage uncertainty in the results given these constraints.

Computable General Equilibrium Models

Like I-O models, CGE models are economywide models. As such, they estimate how economic actors—households, firms, and the government—interact with each other through supply and demand relationships. Both classes of models ultimately have the

---

[9] Rebecca Bess and Zoe O. Ambargis, "Input-Output Models for Impact Analysis: Suggestions for Practitioners Using RIMS II Multipliers," paper presented at the 50th Southern Regional Science Association Conference, New Orleans, La., 2011; Albala-Bertrand, 2014.

[10] C. L. Weber, "Uncertainties in Constructing Environmental Multiregional Input-Output Models," International Input-Output Meeting on Managing the Environment, Seville, Spain, July 9–11, 2008.

[11] Clark W. Bullard and Anthony V. Sebald, "Monte Carlo Sensitivity Analysis of Input-Output Models," *Review of Economics and Statistics*, Vol. 70, No. 4; M. Lenzen, R. Wood, and T. Wiedmann, "Uncertainty Analysis for Multi-Region Input-Output Models—a Case Study of the UK's Carbon Footprint," *Economic Systems Research*, Vol. 22, No. 1, 2010.

same objective: to estimate how changes in certain aspects of the economy affect the broader economy. Such changes may arise because of events like policy changes or natural disasters, which will affect output, prices, and economic incentives. Accordingly, the two sets of models rely on similar forms of data, require similar inputs, and produce similar outputs.

The primary difference lies in how economic interactions are modeled. CGE models are simulation-based optimization models. They simulate economies by optimizing the behavior of each economic actor given budget and resource constraints. For households, this means maximizing welfare (utility) by choosing what and how much to consume given the constraints imposed by income levels and taxation. For firms, this means maximizing profits by choosing amounts of capital, labor, and intermediate inputs subject to their respective prices and the limits of their production processes. The government is often relatively passive in these models, setting taxation levels and redistributing income according to the modeler's choices. Equilibrium in CGE models arises when economywide prices and quantities are such that all markets clear, and each segment of the economy is optimizing given the constraints it faces.

A key implication of this optimization-based structure is that CGE models estimate changes in prices and reactions to those changes. For households, changes in the relative prices of goods and services affect their income and optimal consumption profiles. For firms, price changes affect their chosen inputs to production—capital, labor, and intermediate goods and services—and, consequently, production levels. CGE models therefore contain rational economic behavior that ultimately serves to mitigate the economic effects of a disaster: When certain goods and services become relatively scarce, this affects relative prices, which, in turn, spur households and firms to choose new optimal quantities of consumption, inputs, and outputs. Thus, this class of models is relatively better suited to estimating the effects of longer-term disruptions where such behavior is feasible, plausible, and a significant driver of realized economic effects.

The way in which CGE models project the economic effects of disasters and disaster mitigation activities is conceptually similar to that of I-O models. First, the direct economic effects of a disaster on each sector are estimated. Next, CGE models simulate the resulting relative prices and quantities across markets that characterize the new economic equilibrium. The total and indirect economic effects of the disaster can then be inferred by comparing the initial and subsequent equilibria. Likewise, the projected economic benefits of disaster mitigation efforts are constructed by considering two different prospective before-and-after situations: (1) the economic changes following a disaster when no mitigation efforts occurred and (2) the economic changes following a disaster, given that mitigation efforts did occur before the disaster hit. Comparing economic outcomes across these two scenarios yields the projected economic benefits of the mitigation efforts. If a CGE model is estimated using more granular SAM data, it can also project the economic effects of natural disasters and disaster mitigation on various socioeconomic groups because it explicitly models the household sector.

CGE models have their limitations, some of which are particularly relevant when estimating the indirect economic effects of a natural disaster where identifying the impacts immediately after the event is desirable. This is because CGE models assume that the economy returns to equilibrium, which would likely not happen immediately after the disaster. Without adjustment, the return-to-equilibrium assumption can produce a lower-bound estimate of economic impacts that can be misleading and show a deceivingly resilient postdisaster scenario.[12] Another limitation is the computational complexity of CGE models where computational constraints limit the number of sectors that can be included in the model.[13] Furthermore, failing to capture economic resilience can pose limitations to CGE estimates. Economic resilience occurs when economic actors substitute relatively scarce resources with something else (e.g., if the public water supply is disrupted, using bottled water). Firms can also make up lost income by overworking once the economy has started to recover.[14] Despite these limitations, Yoshio Kajitani and Hirokazu Tatano's (2018) recent validation study shows that CGE estimates of the economic impacts from the 2011 earthquake and tsunami in Japan are consistent with observed production change in both directly and indirectly affected regions.[15] More information on CGE models is contained in Appendix B.[16]

---

[12] Albala-Bertrand, 2014; Adam Rose and Gauri-Shankar Guha, "Computable General Equilibrium Modeling of Electric Utility Lifeline Losses from Earthquakes," in Y. Okuyama and S. E. Chang, eds., *Modeling Spatial and Economic Impacts of Disasters: Advances in Spatial Science*, Berlin: Springer, 2004; Adam Rose and Shu-Yi Liao, "Modeling Regional Economic Resilience to Disasters: A Computable General Equilibrium Analysis of Water Service Disruptions," *Journal of Regional Science*, Vol. 45, No. 1, 2005.

[13] Alex L. Marten and Richard Garbaccio, *An Applied General Equilibrium Model for the Analysis of Environmental Policy: SAGE v1.0 Technical Documentation*, working paper, U.S. Environmental Protection Agency National Center for Environmental Economics, 2018.

[14] Rose and Liao, 2005; Rose and Guha, 2004; Adam Rose, Gbadebo Oladosu, and Shu-Yi Liao, "Business Interruption Impacts of a Terrorist Attack on the Electric Power System of Los Angeles: Customer Resilience to a Total Blackout," *Risk Analysis*, Vol. 27, No. 3, 2007.

[15] Yoshio Kajitani and Hirokazu Tatano, "Applicability of a Spatial Computable General Equilibrium Model to Assess the Short-Term Economic Impact of Natural Disasters," *Economic Systems Research*, Vol. 30, 2017.

[16] The interested reader is also referred to Ian Sue Wing, "Computable General Equilibrium Models for the Analysis of Energy and Climate Policies," in Joanne Evans and Lester C. Hunt, eds., *International Handbook on the Economics of Energy*, Cheltanham, UK: Edward Elgar, 2009.

Findings—Comparative Model Strengths and Weaknesses

Model Accuracy and Breadth

Two key features of the Leontief I-O model limit its usefulness in the disaster recovery context, as well as the usefulness of most other I-O models' variants commonly in use. First, one of the model's key assumptions is that production inputs are not substitutable—particular inputs must be used in particular proportions to produce output. This implies that input proportions do not respond to changes in prices, which contributes to the baseline I-O model being a *static* (as opposed to *dynamic*) model. Static models do not capture time-varying changes in the economic environment or optimal behavioral responses to those changes. It also means that the core model does not capture *economic resilience*—the ability of firms, industries, or regional economies to moderate the realized impacts of a disruption through behavioral responses. I-O models thus may be more desirable for projecting the impacts of short-term disruptions, where price changes and optimizing behavior are either not feasible or not realistic. In general, the static nature of this class of models results in a tendency to produce estimates more reflective of the upper bound of possible disaster impacts. Second, the indirect effects captured by I-O models only include "upstream" or "backward" supply chain effects—the effects of a change in a sector's final output on its direct and indirect suppliers—and not "downstream" or "forward" supply chain effects on the sectors it is a supplier for. This is a consequence of the total requirements matrix—and the technical coefficients matrix from which it is derived—which captures the inputs *to* a given sector that are required for it to produce output. A more complete estimate of indirect economic effects would account for downstream economic effects as well.

These drawbacks of the traditional model and its counterparts can be partially mitigated through two refinements. First, resilience can be incorporated into the model at the sector level in a straightforward manner by using estimated resilience coefficients. The resilience multipliers act to scale the direct effect of a disaster on each industry to produce a disruption that is more representative of the loss each industry is likely to experience, given its estimated ability to attenuate some of the impacts through inherent and adaptive responses. In Appendix B, we illustrate the approach using sector resilience coefficients produced by Rose, Oladosu, and Liao, 2007, which were estimated in the context of a power outage in Los Angeles. Other estimates of sector resilience can be found in the literature; the estimates are somewhat sensitive to the context in which they are estimated. For this reason, it is advisable to obtain sector resilience coefficients for a set of BRIC-relevant disaster scenarios that can then be paired with the approach described in Appendix B.

Second, downstream effects can be captured using an approach similar to Ghosh 1958.[17] The Ghosh approach is methodologically similar to the Leontief I-O approach; the key distinction lies in the assumptions at the heart of each type of model. As noted above, the Leontief I-O model assumes that producers use inputs in fixed proportions. In contrast, the Ghosh approach assumes that sectors send fixed proportions of their output to those sectors that use it as a production input. This slight change to model structure results in a separate (though related) class of models that can be used to estimate downstream effects. Sector resilience can also be incorporated into these models in the same way. See Appendix B for more details on each refinement and the approach we propose for the BRIC program. The approach employs traditional Leontief and Ghosh models that are each augmented to capture sector resilience.

CGE models come with their own set of benefits and drawbacks when it comes to model accuracy and breadth. Their ability to simulate optimizing behavior by consumers and firms better positions them to deal with certain questions than I-O models. Whereas I-O models contain a rigid production and consumption structure, CGE models are more flexible. For example, CGE models capture the effects of changing prices and the behavioral responses of each rational economic actor. This gives CGE models a comparative advantage over I-O models in projecting the economic impacts of a longer-term disruption. However, this capability makes these models less desirable for estimating the impacts of short-term disruptions, when price changes and optimizing behavior may not be possible or realistic. The assumption that consumers and firms are rational, optimizing actors is debatable[18]—particularly in the context of disasters, which create increased uncertainty.[19] Assuming optimizing behavior by all actors results in the models having a tendency to produce estimates closer to the lower bound of possible impacts. CGE models also simultaneously estimate upstream and downstream indirect economic effects, eliminating the need for a separate approach to capture downstream impacts. Moreover, CGE models can leverage SAM data to produce more disaggregated estimates than traditional I-O approaches; for example, CGE models can separate out the effects on different socioeconomic groups. However, exploiting their capability to estimate disaggregated effects or analyze particular sectors comes at the cost of practicality and ease of use, as discussed in the next section. See Appendix B for a discussion of CGE models that could be implemented and used to support the BRIC program.

---

[17] Ambica Ghosh, "Input-Output Approach in an Allocation System," *Economica*, Vol. 25, No. 97, 1958.

[18] Michael R. Greenberg, Michael Lahr, and Nancy Mantell, "Understanding the Economic Costs and Benefits of Catastrophes and Their Aftermath: A Review and Suggestions for the U.S. Federal Government," *Risk Analysis*, Vol. 27, No. 1, 2007.

[19] Yasuhide Okuyama, "Economic Modeling for Disaster Impact Analysis: Past, Present, and Future," *Economic Systems Research*, Vol. 19, No. 2, 2007.

Although each type of model contains certain advantages and disadvantages, it is advisable to use only one model at any given time. In theory, both models could coexist, with an I-O model, for example, being used for projected short-term disruptions and a CGE model being used for longer-term disruptions. However, in practice, it would be difficult to evaluate and compare two different disaster mitigation grant applications whose projected economic effects were estimated using different methodologies with different sets of assumptions.

Practicality and Ease of Use

A significant benefit of the I-O approach is its practicality. The baseline I-O model ultimately only requires the total requirements matrix and projected changes in final output by sector. The BEA publishes the national total requirements matrix at a number of different NAICS industry aggregation levels; this substantially streamlines the process of estimating national-level I-O models.[20] One can also create the total requirements matrix by leveraging the underlying data on interindustry economic flows, which the BEA also publishes at the national level. Regional I-O analysis is, in a broad sense, conducted by "regionalizing" the national-level technical coefficient matrix. This is accomplished through the use of *location quotients*, which compare an industry's concentration within a region to the industry's concentration nationwide. More specifically, a location quotient is calculated by taking the ratio of an industry's share of a regional economic statistic to the industry's share of the corresponding national figure. For most industries, wages and salaries are used to compute location quotients. The location quotients are then used to scale the national technical coefficient matrix to the regional level according to how the industrial concentration within a region differs from its national counterpart. Once the regional technical coefficient matrix has been constructed, standard I-O methods can be applied. The U.S. Bureau of Labor Statistics publishes location quotients down to the county level, which may be downloaded from their webpage.[21] Consequently, I-O models can be easily adapted to a wide range of geographies.

The BEA's Regional Input-Output Modeling System (RIMS II) provides another means to estimate regional economic effects. RIMS II is an I-O framework that also leverages the concept of location quotients to produce economic impact estimates at the regional level. What distinguishes RIMS II is that the model has already been developed and used to produce regional estimates that are succinctly summarized by a set of *multipliers*. The multipliers immediately allow the user to determine how a change in

[20] Specifically, BEA has estimated the total requirements matrix for the 15-, 71-, and 405-industry economies. The different levels of aggregation reflect the hierarchical categorization of industries; that is, the 15-industry economy is expanded into increasingly more specific industry subcategories to produce the matrices for the 71- and 405-industry economies.

[21] U.S. Bureau of Labor Statistics, "Quarterly Census of Employment and Wages: QCEW Location Quotient Details," last updated May 13, 2020.

the final output of one or more industries affects total gross output, value added, earnings, and employment at the regional level. A region is defined as an area consisting of one or more contiguous counties. The ease of use provided by RIMS II comes with a price; at the time of writing this report, RIMS II multipliers cost $275 per region or $75 per industry. Purchasing RIMS II multipliers for a region yields multipliers for all industries within the region, while purchasing multipliers for an industry provides multipliers for that industry for each of the 50 states, plus the District of Columbia. Note that like the Leontief I-O model, the RIMS II model only captures indirect economic effects resulting from "upstream" or "backward" supply chain impacts.

A CGE model can also be fully calibrated using data from the BEA. But exploiting the ability of CGE models to capture more granular effects requires going beyond publicly available BEA data and acquiring SAM data, which are often curated by private entities, such as Impact Analysis for Planning (IMPLAN). Because of the proprietary nature of IMPLAN's data and methods, transparency is limited, including information on validation. In addition, CGE models are more complex than I-O models; this added complexity naturally makes such models more difficult and time-consuming to develop and implement. Also, the fact that CGE models are more technical in nature runs the risk of raising the level of expertise a user needs to have to estimate the economic effects of mitigation projects. Nonetheless, given the degree of overlap between the two in terms of data structure, model inputs, and model outputs, both models largely rest on similar underlying infrastructure.

Ability of Each Method to Leverage the Federal Emergency Management Agency's Hazus Tool

Discussions with FEMA SMEs and former applicants suggest that the technical skill requirements needed to develop a high-quality project proposal are high, relative to the typical knowledge, skills, and experience of applicant staff in some jurisdictions. Such applicants may struggle to master the Benefit Cost Toolkit and provide sufficient technical documentation to support it. They may also struggle to identify promising project candidates. For these applicants, the additional burden of calculating indirect benefits is likely to be onerous.

We explored options for reducing the burden on applicants, and determined that, in principle, an I-O and/or CGE model could be integrated into FEMA's Hazus tool because many indirect benefits model parameters can be drawn from Hazus outputs, while other needed data could be stored in it and the calculations can be automated. Users would still need to supply some model inputs, but the additional applicant burden of calculating indirect benefits and obtaining key data components could potentially be mitigated with this strategy. As an added benefit, automating indirect benefits would contribute to a more level playing field between applicants, who may have unequal access to technically skilled staff.

Two key inputs to I-O models are the projected initial disruption to each sector following a disaster and the estimated sector recovery paths. (See Appendix B for more information.) The initial sectoral disruption in I-O models reflects the expected change in the value of a sector's production of final goods and services over a given time frame—in other words, business interruption losses. Hazus contains a direct economic loss module that estimates, by sector, business interruption losses, the dollar value of building-related direct economic losses, and lifeline infrastructure and transportation systems direct economic losses for a host of disaster scenarios. The business interruption losses component of this module can thus be leveraged in an I-O or CGE model; there are also added benefits to using the Hazus estimates, such as maintaining consistency throughout the disaster planning process.

When translating the Hazus direct economic loss estimates into sectoral disruptions for indirect effects analysis, it is important to distinguish between stock measures versus flow measures. A stock quantity is measured at a point in time, whereas a flow quantity is measured over a given period. I-O and CGE models are both flow models that estimate economic effects over a given time interval. Hence, care needs to be taken to ensure that the direct economic loss figures that are translated into the indirect effects model represent corresponding flow measures. For this reason, business interruption losses are the most appropriate measure to use as the direct economic effect component of either model. Damage to capital equipment or the building stock corresponds to effects on stock measures and hence should be avoided when estimating either model.

Hazus also contains industry restoration functions, which capture the expected recovery path of each industry following a disruption. These can be used in conjunction with Hazus information on lifeline infrastructure recovery times to create projected sector recovery paths for the models. Additionally, the former Hazus indirect economic loss module, which has been inactive for some time, was designed to accept user-supplied SAM data from IMPLAN. Given the high level of similarity between SAM and I-O data,[22] we assume that adapting the previous framework to accept I-O or CGE model data is relatively straightforward.

Summary

Indirect consequences reflect the economic impacts on those who are connected to businesses and lifeline infrastructure that are directly affected by a disaster. When estimating the degree to which hazard mitigation projects are expected to benefit the broader community, it is imperative to account for indirect consequences because the economic impacts of a disaster may be predominantly indirect. The approach we used

---

[22] C. Stahmer, "Social Accounting Matrices and Extended Input-Output Tables," in OECD, *Measuring Sustainable Development: Integrated Economic, Environmental and Social Frameworks*, Paris: OECD, 2004.

to determine suitable methods for projecting indirect benefits in the context of the BRIC program contained two phases. First, we reviewed the existing literature to identify methodologies appropriate for estimating the economic effects of natural disasters and mitigation projects; this review established I-O models and CGE models as possible approaches. Second, we weighed the benefits and drawbacks to each approach against the backdrop provided by the BRIC program.

Our analysis informed a number of findings. A notable advantage of the I-O approach is its practicality, which itself consists of a number of dimensions. First, I-O models are less technically complex than CGE models. Second, the approach generalizes in a way that makes it straightforward to apply consistently across SLTTs. Third, the approach can rely on publicly available data. Fourth, the approach's relative simplicity requires users to have comparatively lower technical expertise. Moreover, the approach is well suited to estimating the impacts of shorter-term disruptions. CGE models can also be fully calibrated using publicly available data and contain certain advantages over I-O models. Their ability to capture price effects and optimal firm and consumer responses make them more suitable for estimating the effects of longer-term disruptions. The models can also leverage SAM data to provide more disaggregated estimates than traditional I-O approaches. While CGE models are more complex than I-O models, both models ultimately rest on similar underlying infrastructure given the extent of overlap between the two in data structure, model inputs, and model outputs. Each model could also be integrated into Hazus as a relatively automated component and leverage Hazus's existing capabilities to calibrate some key model inputs.

CHAPTER FOUR

Applicant Institutional Capacity Line of Effort

Introduction

This LoE researched how AIC—the set of assets and capabilities that enables applicants to effectively propose and manage mitigation grants—might affect the benefits that hazard mitigation projects are expected to provide. A number of AIC factors affect project performance, such as prior experience with hazard mitigation grants, size and capacity of the relevant state hazard mitigation office, and access to technical expertise. When all other circumstances are similar, reduced AIC might either result in increased costs to complete the project or in decreased expected benefits from the project. Both increased costs and decreased expected benefits diminish the project's expected benefit/cost ratio. The interactions between AIC, indirect benefits (Chapter Three), and community resilience (Chapter Five) are also important considerations for BRIC grant decisionmaking.

To address this topic, the HSOAC team (1) drew insights from select documents relevant to institutional capacity to generally inform our interview protocol; (2) interviewed 11 SMEs with experience executing mitigation grants or working with grant applicants; and (3) developed an assessment scorecard to help decisionmakers evaluate applicant performance potential. Evaluation of AIC could ultimately support technical assistance or tiered competition decisionmaking. The remainder of this chapter describes the evaluation methods and the findings/implications of this LoE.

Methods

Insights from Institutional Capacity Literature

The HSOAC research team sought insights from the institutional capacity literature to inform the development of the AIC interview protocol. HSOAC first identified three broad literatures that could be useful for protocol development: (1) literature on local, state, and federal capacity to manage and implement federal grants programs, including grants for disaster mitigation and response; (2) literature on conditions and barriers that influence adaptive capacity to climate change and extreme weather events;

and (3) literature on institutional capacity building in the international development context.

Literature on local, state, and federal capacity challenges is extensive, spanning topics related to securing, managing, and implementing federal grants. Some of this literature focuses on local government, exploring the various capacity dimensions—such as human resources and financing—that influence a local government's ability to compete for and administer grants.[1] Other literature examines the state's role in building and supporting local capacity to plan for and implement federal grants, including those for hazard mitigation.[2] Some authors have explored issues and challenges at the federal level with management and implementation of grant programs intended to support state and local governments, such as FEMA's disaster mitigation, response, and recovery grant programs.[3] The grant programs examined in this literature go beyond FEMA programs to include other federal programs that may deliver postdisaster federal assistance, such as the Community Development Block Grant (CDBG) program administered by the U.S. Department of Housing and Urban Development.[4]

Literature on adaptive capacity and resilience to extreme weather events, disasters, and stresses related to climate change is voluminous. This research examines what factors make individuals, communities, and governments more or less vulnerable to disasters and more or less able to adapt and respond to them.[5] The literature includes efforts to identify and measure characteristics that increase capacity for disaster resilience[6] and case studies examining disaster resilience at the community level.[7] The research

---

[1] See, for example, Jeremy L. Hall, "Assessing Local Capacity for Federal Grant Getting," *American Review of Public Administration*, Vol. 38, No. 4, December 2008.

[2] Gavin Smith, Ward Lyles, and Philip Berke, "The Role of the State in Building Local Capacity and Commitment for Hazard Mitigation Planning," *International Journal of Mass Emergencies and Disasters*, Vol. 31, No. 2, August 2013; Ward Lyles, Philip Berke, and Gavin Smith, "A Comparison of Local Hazard Mitigation Plan Quality in Six States," *Landscape and Urban Planning*, Vol. 122, 2014.

[3] See, for instance, Patrick S. Roberts, *Disasters and the American State: How Politicians, Bureaucrats, and the Public Prepare for the Unexpected*, New York: Cambridge University Press, 2013.

[4] See, for instance, Jonathan Spader and Jennifer Turnham, "CDBG Disaster Recovery Assistance and Homeowners' Rebuilding Outcomes Following Hurricanes Katrina and Rita," *Housing Policy Debate*, Vol. 24, January 2014.

[5] See, for instance, Barry Smit and Johanna Wandel, "Adaptation, Adaptive Capacity and Vulnerability," *Global Environmental Change*, Vol. 16, 2006; Yiheyis Taddele Maru, Mark Stafford Smith, Ashley Sparrow, Patricia F. Pinho, and Opha Pauline Dube, "A Linked Vulnerability and Resilience Framework for Adaptation Pathways in Remote Disadvantaged Communities," *Global Environmental Change*, Vol. 28, 2014.

[6] Susan L. Cutter, Christopher G. Burton, and Christopher T. Emrich, "Disaster Resilience Indicators for Benchmarking Baseline Conditions," *Journal of Homeland Security and Emergency Management*, Vol. 7, No. 1, 2010.

[7] John J. Kiefer, Monica T. Farris, and Natalie Durel, "Building Internal Capacity for Community Disaster Resiliency by Using a Collaborative Approach: A Case Study of the University of New Orleans

on adaptive capacity has also sought to develop frameworks for understanding barriers to climate change adaptation[8] and to identify limits—whether cultural, economic, or otherwise—to adaptive capacity.[9] Other literature has explored how governance and policy interventions may be able to reduce vulnerability to disaster or climate change stresses at the local or national level.[10]

Finally, the HSOAC research team identified literature from the international development field related to institutional capacity building, including a number of capacity frameworks, academic papers, and practitioner-oriented guides. Because these resources offered high-level, generalizable findings about the nature and characteristics of institutional capacity, HSOAC further examined a limited sample of the international development literature. These findings were useful in drawing out general capacity factors across institutional settings, including for FEMA grant applicants. HSOAC's examination of the international development literature was not intended to be comprehensive, given the wide range of relevant publications, but rather to provide general insights into the major institutional capacity factors that may be applicable to SLTT governments in the domestic hazard mitigation context. Specifically, insights from the international development literature served two purposes. First, it provided the research team with a general understanding of how institutional capacity is defined and measured in the field of international development. While institutional capacity among SLTT governments in the United States is not the same as institutional capacity among developing nations, many of the key considerations are similar. Thus, insights from the international development literature can provide lessons learned that have analogous parallels in our context. Second, it offered additional insights to be included in our interview protocol for eliciting AIC knowledge from SMEs who were applicants or who worked with applicants.

To identify relevant literature, we reviewed websites of public institutions with major roles in international development, including the World Bank, the U.S. Agency for International Development (USAID), and the United Nations Development Programme (UNDP). Extending this convenience sample, we then used a snowball approach to identify additional resources based on sources cited by these public institutions. We also conducted keyword searches using Google, Google Scholar, and the

---

Disaster Resistant University Project," *Journal of Emergency Management*, Vol. 4, No. 2, March/April 2006.

[8] Susanne C. Moser and Julia Ekstrom, "A Framework to Diagnose Barriers to Climate Change Adaptation," *Proceedings of the National Academy of Sciences of the United States of America*, Vol. 107, No. 51, December 2010.

[9] W. Neil Adger, Suraje Dessai, Marisa Goulden, Mike Hulme, Irene Lorenzoni, Donald R. Nelson, Lars Otto Naess, Johanna Wolf, and Anita Wreford, "Are There Social Limits to Adaptation to Climate Change?" *Climatic Change*, Vol. 93, 2009.

[10] W. Neil Adger, "Vulnerability," *Global Environmental Change*, Vol. 16, 2006.

Web of Science database to search for additional literature. Appendix C contains further discussion of the sources identified by the convenience sampling.

Interview Methods to Identify Important Applicant Institutional Capacity Factors

We conducted semistructured interviews with FEMA SMEs to (1) identify factors that bolster or impede AIC and (2) determine how AIC affects project performance. The data collection process involved developing the interview protocol, conducting interviews with FEMA SMEs, qualitatively coding their responses, and analyzing the results to provide inputs to an AIC assessment scorecard.

Creating Interview Protocol for Structured Applicant Institutional Capacity Investigation

To prepare for the interviews, the research team drew insights from a limited sample of the international development literature and practitioner-oriented guidance (as described below in the Findings section and detailed in Appendix C) to identify factors that contribute to or hinder effective government institutions. This provided additional insights to be included in the development of our interview protocol (Appendix D).

Conducting 11 Federal Emergency Management Agency Subject-Matter Expert Interviews to Elicit Important Applicant Institutional Capacity Factors

We asked 11 FEMA SMEs a set of main questions with relevant probing, in accordance with funnel design best practice. Analogous to a funnel, this involved posing broad questions of interest first, followed by more specific probes. Questions were asked about the SMEs' relevant roles, how they think about successful project completion based on their knowledge and experience,[11] what traits successful applicants possess, the most important factors that influence applicant capacity to complete projects, and the challenges and opportunities to improve on-time and on-budget project completion (Appendix D). The HSOAC team conducted interviews by telephone that lasted approximately 90 minutes each. We interviewed a total of 11 FEMA experts.

Qualitative Coding Process and Analysis of Federal Emergency Management Agency Subject-Matter Expert Interviews

Our analytical approach involved qualitatively coding the expert interviews and identifying emergent themes. We developed a codebook through iteration with the research team to capture what experts believe influences AIC and the relationship between AIC and project performance (Appendix E). While each interview was coded for major

---

[11] Project performance was evaluated for on-time and on-budget project completion in SME interviews. However, some SMEs defined project success differently; such differences included completing scope of work, loss-avoidance demonstrating mitigation value, and the quality of the application or project work.

themes, the focus was on identifying traits or internal factors that contribute to high-capacity applicants.

We used a general three-step process for coding interview responses:

1. Evaluate each individual interview response.
2. Identify and code whether the SME is describing high- or low-capacity applicants.
3. Within each high-capacity excerpt, code traits or internal factors that contribute to high-capacity applicants, according to the SME.

Using Dedoose, a content analysis tool, we calculated statistics on how often each respondent mentioned each factor, how many respondents mentioned each factor, and how often respondents mentioned each possible pair of factors in the same interview excerpt.[12] These statistics informed the development of the AIC assessment scorecard.

Federal Emergency Management Agency Subject-Matter Expert Responses Inform the Creation of a Scorecard

To create a scorecard, we distilled categories of questions from the SME interviews that encapsulated the most frequently mentioned traits of high-capacity applicants and then developed concrete questions from them in consultation with a FEMA SME. This resulted in a 12-question scorecard that evaluated four categories of frequently mentioned traits.

Findings

This section discusses our findings. First, we identify four factors that contribute to institutional capacity—organization and procedures, leadership, motivated and skilled workforce, and material resources—drawn from general international development insights to inform our interview protocol. Next, we review the findings from our interviews, determining that workforce matters most in the AIC context. Then, we show the results of using the interview results to create the scorecard. Finally, we discuss some comparisons between the insights drawn from the international development literature and SME interview findings.

Insights from Institutional Capacity Literature

Our limited examination of documents relevant to institutional capacity identified scholarly research and practitioner-oriented guidance on institutional capacity—both what constitutes it and how to bolster it. The literature we reference included several frameworks and approaches for understanding institutional capacity. (See Appendix C for a larger discussion.) Although these approaches diverge in terminology and points

---

12 Frequency data were weighted for each interview by dividing code prevalence by the number of excerpts in the respective interview, so as to not under-/overweight shorter/longer interviews.

of emphasis, there is considerable overlap in their description of the basic features of institutional capacity.

In particular, we identified four key factors that contribute to institutional capacity: (1) organization and procedures, (2) leadership, (3) a motivated and skilled workforce, and (4) material resources. These four factors align closely with the DHS Doctrine, Organization, Training, Materiel, Leadership, Personnel, Facilities plus Regulations, Grants, and Standards (DOTMLPF+R/G/S) framework, a DHS decision support tool that lists fundamental organizational requirements for successful operations.[13] Table 4.1 provides examples of the four key capacity factors and crosswalks them to the DHS DOTMLPF+R/G/S framework. As noted above, we later drew on this four-factor general framework when developing the semistructured interview protocol.

Creating the Scorecard from Interview Results

FEMA SMEs identified an appropriately trained and skilled workforce (n = 11), prior experience (n = 11), access to management (n = 8), and technical capabilities (n = 7) as the most important internal factors for high-performing applicants. This translated into four broad categories for evaluating AIC.[14]

The results of the SME interviews and scorecard creation findings are reflected in Table 4.2, which shows the resulting four categories of frequently mentioned traits to evaluate those criteria (Table 4.2).

Table 4.1
Institutional Capacity Factors Derived from Examining Select Documents

Factor	Example	DOTMLPF+R/G/S Framework
Organization and procedures	Designated roles and responsibilities, standard operating procedures, unity of effort, quality management, anticorruption controls	Doctrine, organization, standards
Leadership	Strategic vision, continuity over time	Leadership
Workforce	Skilled and motivated workers, training, experience	Training, personnel
Material resources	Funds, equipment, facilities	Materiel, facilities

[13] Michael Vasseur, Dwayne M. Butler, Brandon Crosby, Benjamin N. Harris, and Christopher Scott Adams, *An Assessment of the Joint Requirements Council's (JRC) Organization and Staffing*, Homeland Security Operational Analysis Center operated by the RAND Corporation, RR-2473-DHS, 2018.

[14] Note that FEMA SMEs tended to focus on proximate factors for high-performing applicants (e.g., a highly trained workforce) as opposed to potentially higher-level factors that may influence applicant performance (e.g., government budget constraints).

Table 4.2
Applicant Institutional Capacity Evaluation Criterion Categories

Evaluation Criterion Category	Criterion for Evaluating AIC
Staff retention[a]	**General staff turnover:** On average, applicant retains staff for many years. **Key staff turnover:** Applicant typically retains key staff for many years; key staff retention rate is generally higher than its general staff retention rate. Key staff include those with relevant roles and responsibilities, such as grant writers, project managers, technical leads, and personnel with decision authority. If the applicant has a relatively small staff (or even just one), all would be considered "key" staff.
Staff skill	**Expertise:** Staff completed training for predisaster mitigation work. Relevant training is contingent on needs of proposed work/project. Examples include hazard mitigation assistance introductory courses (i.e., 212, 213, and 214) or similar; benefit-cost analysis training (e.g., 276) or similar; grant management training; certifications for key staff, defined in the staff retention evaluation criteria.
Staff experience	**Experience:** Applicant's lead SME has many years of experience with predisaster mitigation grants.
Management and technical capabilities	**Management:** Applicant has all the administrative capabilities needed to manage grants, including financial and contractor management. **Technical:** Applicant has access to technical expertise—engineering, benefit-cost analysis, project time/cost estimation, and so on.

[a] While staff turnover criteria are an important factor according to FEMA SMEs, such criteria could inadvertently penalize an organization with a younger or more mobile staff, irrespective of organization capability. In general, we encourage decisionmakers to think of these criteria as opportunities for providing targeted technical assistance support to applicants rather than as merit criteria for judging applications.

A recommended scorecard that uses the evaluation criteria from Table 4.2 is given in Figure 4.1. Criteria are displayed in rank order of importance, according to FEMA SMEs (i.e., criteria at the top of the scorecard were more often cited as important than criteria toward the bottom). However, a weighting scheme for these criteria was not elicited during the interview process.

More yeses in the AIC assessment scorecard indicate higher applicant capacity. Applicants might address shortfalls by focusing on staffing retention, training, hiring, and reliable access to expertise. BRIC technical assistance might support this by making expertise more widely available, perhaps by (1) providing or subsidizing specialized consultants for all applicants who meet a minimum preliminary standard, (2) facilitating staff resource pooling across many jurisdictions, or (3) independently identifying high-value potential projects for applicants, so they can submit targeted applications.

Figure 4.1
Applicant Institutional Capacity Evaluation Scorecard

Evaluation Criterion	Yes/No
Staff retention: Do these types of staff generally stay for at least eight years?	
Staff with grant writing responsibilities	
Staff with mitigation grant management responsibilities	
Technical leads	
Staff with decision authority	
Staff skill and experience: Do at least two staff members possess these qualifications?	
Completed hazard mitigation assistance introductory courses (212, 213, 214) or similar	
Completed benefit-cost analysis training course (276) or similar	
Completed grant management training	
Five years of experience with predisaster mitigation grants	
Management capability: Does the organization have these established procedures?	
Procedure for managing contractors	
Procedure for financial management	
Technical capability: Does the organization have reliable access to these kinds of contractors?	
Engineering firms	
Construction firms	

NOTE: Specific numbers are just placeholders. FEMA should set numbers, based on statistics typical of high-performing applicants. Statistics can be gathered as part of the application process.

Comparing Insights from the International Development Literature and Interview Findings

Our comparison of institutional capacity key factors from the international development literature with those mentioned in FEMA interviews revealed several areas of convergence. A common theme from the international development literature and from FEMA interviews was the importance of building an appropriately skilled and resourced workforce. Like much practitioner-oriented guidance in the international context, FEMA experts frequently mentioned the importance of having sufficient staff capacity to handle and manage the workload in public-sector organizations. Similarly, FEMA experts and the international development literature both stressed the importance of human capital factors, such as professional experience, institutional knowledge, technical proficiency, and employee motivation.

Differences in emphasis between the international development literature and FEMA interviews were often linked to the significantly different material and institutional conditions in which public-sector organizations in the developing world and the United States operate. For instance, the international development literature was more focused on securing the basic material resources that organizations need to sustain operations. In addition, the international development literature was more focused on building rule-based public-sector organizations that are free from corruption and undue outside influence. In contrast, FEMA experts more frequently mentioned the importance of employee retention and the negative impact of turnover. This may be because the U.S. labor market offers more attractive alternatives for public-sector employees than those available to government employees in lower-income settings. Finally, the international development literature was more oriented toward general institutional capacity factors than FEMA experts, who tended to highlight specific areas of technical expertise, such as engineering, benefit-cost analysis, and project management, that are critical in the predisaster mitigation grant context.

Other Considerations for Evaluating Applicant Institutional Capacity

The primary objective of this LoE was to provide a structured guide for assessing applicant capacity to inform BRIC decisionmaking. In our interviews, FEMA SMEs also mentioned other factors that influence project performance, including those outside the applicant's control and opportunities to improve overall capacity.

Federal Emergency Management Agency Subject-Matter Experts Identified External Applicant Institutional Capacity Influencers Outside the Applicant's Control

FEMA experts provided insights into a range of external factors that affect an applicant's ability to submit grant applications and to complete projects on time and on budget. The most frequently mentioned external factor was disaster activity. Since applicant staff often work on both predisaster mitigation and disaster response and recovery, disaster events can divert applicant staff from mitigation work and delay project completion. Weather was the second most frequently mentioned external factor. Several FEMA experts noted that weather conditions, like heavy rainfall, could slow project completion; others pointed out that harsh winter conditions in some project sites could lead to shortened construction seasons. Many FEMA experts said that the complexity of federal grant programs, demanding environmental and historic preservation requirements, and funding delays at the state and federal levels could also slow or stall progress. Other factors beyond the applicant's control included economic conditions that can influence prices or contractor availability and community socioeconomic traits that can influence the level of resources available to the applicant.

Federal Emergency Management Agency Subject-Matter Experts Identified Improvement Opportunities

In addition to offering insights on applicant capacity factors, FEMA SMEs also offered ideas for improvement, focusing primarily on performance. Table 4.3 summarizes these opportunities as (1) investing in more rigorous risk assessments, (2) widespread adoption of disaster resistance codes, (3) greater transparency in the grant award process, (4) incentive programs, (5) fostering partnerships between applicants and FEMA, and (6) using the Community Rating System (CRS) and Building Code Effectiveness Grading Schedule (BCEGS) as first-order capacity indicators.[15]

Table 4.3
Suggestion Box: Other Areas for Improvement

Improvement Opportunity	Specific Suggestion
Risk assessments	"If you don't know your risks, you're not in a good position to play. So, [understanding] what are the hazards, what are our mitigation options . . . I know risk assessments are included in hazard mitigation plans, but a lot of time these are just seen as checked boxes."—SME 11
Mitigation	"We might get more impact by pushing disaster-resistant codes than by sprinkling funding around for mitigation projects. Because there isn't enough money for mitigation projects to go around. If we can get states and local governments to take ownership of adopting disaster-resistant codes, that could make a difference."—SME 5
Transparency	"In terms of transparency, we could be more transparent, and that would help people in the process. Ever ordered something from Dominos? Something like that could be good. We made your pizza, it's cooking, it's on the way. It'd be helpful for them to know if they're getting funding in two months or two years. It would be helpful for them to start staging."—SME 4
Incentives	"If there's some way to reward communities for their capacity, or to reward those that have, say, managed three cycles with no reporting or violation, by awarding 5 percent more funding during the next cycle. . . . Maybe FEMA can use incentives to help with staff retention. Or just talking and having an open dialogue with states about what's inhibiting them and thinking of ways to help."—SME 3
Partnerships	"[Applicants] could reach out to the state or to the federal government, whichever they're applying to, and communicate. Put the pride aside. If you don't know, ask. Think of it as a partnership. 'Oh, the feds are in charge. We can't talk to them; they're big scary people.' It's doing it more as a team."—SME 7
Indicators	"Communities with a high BCEGS score have better capacity. . . . States and local governments with higher CRS scores and higher BCEGS scores—those are other indicators of states that are better at putting together higher-quality applications."—SME 5

[15] CRS and BCEGS are discussed in detail in Chapter Five.

Summary

We informally reviewed select documents relevant to institutional capacity, performed 11 FEMA SME interviews, and developed an AIC assessment scorecard. Our synthesis of the interview responses underscored that the most important internal factors for high-performing applicants were an appropriately trained and skilled workforce, prior experience, and access to management and technical capabilities. The specific evaluation criteria include general and key staff turnover, staff skill/expertise and prior experience with predisaster mitigation projects and grants, management/administration capabilities, and access to technical expertise to propose predisaster mitigation projects.

In addition to internal factors, FEMA SMEs in our interviews also mentioned external factors outside an applicant's control that influence project performance, such as disaster activity and weather delays. FEMA SMEs offered additional suggestions for improvement, including a better understanding of risks, adoption of disaster resistance codes, transparent grant award processes, incentives, FEMA partnerships, and using existing measures, like CRS and BCEGS, as capacity indicators.

CHAPTER FIVE

Community Resilience Line of Effort

Introduction

The third LoE focused on community resilience. This concept recognizes that some communities are more robust to disasters than others and that mitigation projects strive to bolster this robustness. In contrast to the other LoEs, resilience is a common concept at FEMA. FEMA has a deputy administrator for resilience, whose office oversees FEMA's activities to sustain continuity, encourage insurance, mitigate the negative consequences of natural disasters, and bolster preparedness. FEMA has also periodically commissioned the Argonne National Laboratory to conduct research into peer-reviewed resilience metrics, most recently in 2019.[1]

However, the BRIC program faces two challenges for community resilience measurement. First, many community resilience metrics focus on attributes that a BRIC grant cannot change and, therefore, do not provide a viable performance evaluation benchmark for the program. For example, the Argonne report cites religious affiliation as a community resilience factor. However, the First Amendment of the Constitution prohibits Congress from "respecting an establishment of religion, or prohibiting the free exercise thereof,"[2] so BRIC grants cannot fund initiatives to increase community religious affiliation to bolster community resilience. BRIC-funded interventions targeting many common community resilience indicators—age, single-parent households, unemployment, and so on—raise legal, practical, ethical, and/or feasibility challenges. Second, many community resilience indicators are already in use at FEMA. Introducing new measures may be counterproductive if it detracts from efforts to converge on a common understanding of community resilience and how to measure it. For this reason, our sponsor requested that we focus on metrics already in use.

Given these challenges, we devised a three-pronged approach to supporting BRIC's community resilience measurement needs. First, we researched and described each of ten measures currently in use. Second, we developed a customized evaluation

1 FEMA, "Community Resilience Indicator Analysis: County-Level Analysis of Commonly Used Indicators from Peer-Reviewed Research," November 2019b.

2 U.S. Constitution, Amendment I.

framework for FEMA to use to understand the relative merits of each metric and to evaluate metrics not currently use. This framework was customized to BRIC's needs in that it considered Stafford Act Section 203 directives, as well as whether BRIC grants could potentially affect scores. Third, we conducted a test run of the framework, having two HSOAC SMEs use it to assess each of the ten metrics. This test run was not intended to produce the final word on the merits of each metric. Instead, it was intended to demonstrate how to use the framework and highlight important decisionmaker considerations for conducting community resilience measurement.

The remainder of this chapter describes the methods and the findings/implications of this LoE.

Methods

As noted above, the concept of resilience is prevalent in FEMA doctrine and organization. However, this important concept is not defined in the DHS Risk Lexicon,[3] and hundreds of definitions could be used.[4] After discussions with FEMA leadership, we chose the National Institute of Standards and Technology (NIST) definition highlighted in a previously funded FEMA study.[5] According to NIST, the definition of community resilience is as follows: "[C]ommunity resilience is the ability to prepare for anticipated hazards, adapt to changing conditions, and withstand and recover rapidly from disruptions. Activities, such as disaster preparedness—which includes prevention, protection, mitigation, response and recovery—are key steps to resilience."[6] Generally speaking, this means community resilience may have the ability to reduce the costs of hazardous events (and thus demonstrate cost savings to the DRF) by making communities resistant to disaster disruption.

Starting with the above definition, HSOAC searched FEMA websites and documents to identify "off-the-shelf" metrics currently in use at FEMA, read peer-reviewed documentation about each measure, created a scorecard to help a decisionmaker choose between those metrics, and conducted a test run of the scorecard rankings (using two HSOAC SMEs).

To create a scorecard, we considered categories of questions to score potential methods to measure community resilience. After choosing the categories, we conducted multiple discussions (both internal to the HSOAC team, as well as with FEMA

---

[3] Risk Steering Committee, 2010.

[4] Craig A. Bond, Aaron Strong, Nicholas Burger, Sarah Weilant, Uzaib Saya, and Anita Chandra, *Resilience Dividend Valuation Model Framework Development and Initial Case Studies*, Santa Monica, Calif.: RAND Corporation, RR-2129-RF, 2017.

[5] FEMA, 2019c.

[6] NIST, "Community Resilience," webpage, undated.

SMEs) to choose high-level merit criteria that fit these categories. For each merit criterion, two HSOAC SMEs created a longer definition of what would and would not meet the criterion.

Two HSOAC SMEs used the developed scorecard to independently rate the chosen "off-the-shelf" community resilience metrics in a test run. After separately rating the metrics, the SMEs compared results and adjudicated differences. The results discuss both the final adjudicated result and areas of differences.

Findings

Here we present the findings derived from the review of metric documentation and the creation of the scorecard.

Review of Select Community Resilience Measure Documentation

We first began with reviews of the literature that had already been completed.[7] One review of the existing literature suggested that there are multiple frameworks that could be used to define resilience, such as Maslow's hierarchy of needs;[8] such frameworks also included those that (1) reduce the likelihood of a disaster and a community's ability to absorb or resist a shock, (2) increase a system's adaptability while still maintaining function in the presence of a shock, and (3) reduce the time to recovery to normal functioning that might differ from pre-event functioning.[9] After discussions with the sponsor, we chose the NIST definition of community resilience (as given in the Introduction).

Then, given that the existing literature is replete with measures and many of them are already in use at FEMA, we focused on evaluating the "off-the-shelf" metrics thought to be in use at FEMA and considered them in terms of how useful they are in the BRIC environment. Our review focused on "off-the-shelf" metrics in use at FEMA, for both hazard-agnostic and hazard-specific approaches.

---

[7] For example, National Research Council, *Disaster Resilience: A National Imperative*, Washington, D.C.: National Academies Press, 2012; M. Doherty, K. Klima, and J. Hellmann, "Climate Change in the Urban Environment: Advancing, Measuring, and Achieving Resiliency," *Environmental Science and Policy*, Vol. 66, 2016; Aaron Strong and Debra Knopman, *Landscape Survey to Support Flood Apex National Flood Decision Support Toolbox: Definitions and Existing Tools*, Santa Monica, Calif.: RAND Corporation, RR-1933-UNC, 2017.

[8] Abraham Harold Maslow, "A Theory of Human Motivation," *Psychological Review*, Vol. 50, No. 4, 1943, p. 370.

[9] Strong and Knopman, 2017.

Hazard-Agnostic Ways to Measure Community Resilience

This section describes some of the commonly known approaches to measuring community resilience (summarized at the end of the section in Table 5.1). These measures are discussed in more detail below.

Community Resilience Indicator Analysis and Resilience Analysis and Planning Tool

Given the wealth of possible approaches to community resilience, in 2018, FEMA tasked the Argonne National Laboratory with conducting research on how to define and measure community resilience. According to the Executive Summary of the November 2019 Update:[10]

> To begin the 2018 analysis, the Argonne research team first conducted a literature review to identify meta-analyses of peer-reviewed community resilience assessment methodologies published within the past five years. This search identified six relevant meta-analyses. Next, the research team reviewed the six meta-analyses to catalog each distinct assessment methodology they referenced, ultimately identifying 73 distinct methodologies. Argonne then reviewed these 73 methodologies and retained those that met the following criteria: they used a unit of analysis that corresponded to U.S. county-level data, applied to multiple hazards, had a predisaster focus, used quantitative measures, used a publicly available methodology, and used publicly available data sources. Applying these criteria narrowed the pool of methodologies to eight.
>
> The research team then identified more than 100 quantitative indicators used within these eight methodologies and selected only those indicators cited in three or more methodologies. This process resulted in 20 indicators, 11 with a population focus and 9 with a community focus.
>
> Fifteen of the 20 indicators use census 5-year average data.

The authors called this the Community Resilience Indicator Analysis (CRIA) and Resilience Analysis and Planning Tool. In addition to this specific metric, the report served as an excellent FEMA-funded literature review of community resilience. As a result, many of that report's highlighted measures are listed again below in this study.

[10] FEMA, 2019c.

Social Vulnerability Index (SoVI)

FEMA's National Risk Index uses the Social Vulnerability Index (SoVI).[11] The SoVI[12] assigns social vulnerability scores at the U.S. county level using 1990 data that were recalculated in 2000, 2005–2009, and 2006–2010. The authors' approach was originally based on the Hazards-of-Place model, with 42 vulnerability measures based on census data. Through factor analysis, the 42 vulnerability measures were reduced to 11 factors—including personal wealth, age, density of built environment, single-sector economic dependence, housing stock, race, ethnicity, occupation, and infrastructure dependence—in order of percentage of variance. Each factor was normalized, equally weighted, and summed in the composite SoVI. High SoVI scores indicate high vulnerability, which was evident in areas of the rural south and along the Mississippi River. Some of the least vulnerable areas (i.e., those with low SoVI scores) are evident in coastal areas across the Southeast and some counties on the East Coast. This metric was not empirically validated by its authors. SoVI has been shown to be valid in the Gulf Coast region for predicting damages and disaster declarations in Gulf states, although the sign for damages is opposite from expected (more vulnerable locations are experiencing fewer damages).[13] The test of validation against fatalities was not statistically significant.

Social Vulnerability Index (SVI)

Building on previous research by Flanagan et al., 2011,[14] Geospatial Research, Analysis, and Services Program of the Centers for Disease Control and Prevention (CDC) developed a Social Vulnerability Index (SVI).[15] Currently, SVI estimates are available for the years 2000, 2010, 2014, and 2016. SVI assigns social vulnerability scores at the U.S. census-tract level using a percentile ranking approach for 15 variables, excluding the 2010 estimate that does not include disability data.

SVI uses the following variables: (1) below poverty level, (2) unemployment status, (3) income, (4) no high school diploma, (5) age 65 or older, (6) age 17 or younger, (7) older than age 5 with a disability, (8) single-parent households, (9) minority status, (10) nonfluent English, (11) multiunit housing, (12) mobile homes, (13) level of residential crowding, (14) no vehicle, and (15) group quarters. Each of these variables

---

[11] FEMA, *FEMA's National Risk Index*, Washington, D.C.: FEMA, undated a.

[12] S. L. Cutter, B. J. Boruff, and L. W. Shirley, "Social Vulnerability to Environmental Hazards," *Social Science Quarterly*, Vol. 84, No. 2, 2003.

[13] Laura A. Bakkensen, Cate Fox-Lent, Laura K. Read, and Igor Linkov, "Validating Resilience and Vulnerability Indices in the Context of Natural Disasters," *Risk Analysis*, Vol. 37, no. 5, 2017.

[14] B. Flanagan, E. Gregory, E. Hallisey, J. Heitgerd, and B. Lewis, "A Social Vulnerability Index for Disaster Management," *Journal of Homeland Security and Emergency Management*, Vol. 8, No. 1, 2011.

[15] Elaine J. Hallisey, "Measuring Community Vulnerability to Natural and Anthropogenic Hazards: The Centers for Disease Control and Prevention's Social Vulnerability Index," *Journal of Environmental Health*, Vol. 80, No. 10, 2018.

was ranked from highest to lowest vulnerability for each U.S. census tract, followed by a percentile rank calculation for each. Variables were then grouped into four broader themes: (1) socioeconomic status, (2) household composition and disability, (3) minority status and language, and (4) housing and transportation status. A percentile rank calculation was then performed for each tract for each of the four broader themes, followed by an overall, summative percentile ranking for each tract. Mapping of these results shows potentially high social vulnerability, particularly across the southeast and southwest United States. SVI has been shown to be valid in the Gulf Coast region for predicting damages and fatalities.[16]

Community Disaster Resilience Index

The Community Disaster Resilience Index (CDRI)[17] is a composite index that assigns community resilience scores to 144 coastal (or near-coastal) Gulf State counties using data from 2000 to 2005. While only applied in the Gulf region, the Argonne Laboratory 2019 report included CDRI in its inclusion criteria since it "could be easily adapted to a U.S. county level."[18] The authors' matrix approach is based on a final set of 75 indicators binned into four capital domains—social, economic, physical, and human—and across four disaster phases: mitigation, preparedness, response, and recovery. The four capital domains and four disaster phases comprise 16 matrix cells. The methodology classified an initial set of 120 variables into the 16 matrix cells. Then, the authors used alpha analysis for internal consistency to maximize alpha within each cell using the fewest number of variables. This analysis resulted in the final 75 indicators across the four capital domains, including 9, 6, 35, and 25 indicators of social, economic, physical, and human capital indicators, respectively. For the final composite CDRI, individual metric scores were z normalized to center the average at zero, because the indicators occurred in various forms (e.g., percentages, means, medians); then, all indicators within each of the four capital resource categories were averaged; and finally, the four capital indices were averaged to compute CDRI. CDRI ranges from –1.3 (least resilient) to 1.4 (most resilient). The southern horn of Texas showed a cluster of low-resilient counties compared to more resilient areas, like Houston, and Gulf counties in Florida. The authors provide empirical validation of CDRI using correlations and regressions for predicting disaster losses and fatalities. CDRI performed well overall, except for probability of death. In addition, CDRI has been shown to be valid in the Gulf Coast region for predicting damages and fatalities; the test of valida-

16 Bakkensen et al., 2017.

17 W. Peacock, S. Brody, W. Seitz, W. Merrell, A. Vedlitz, S. Zahran, R. Harriss, and R. Stickney, *Advancing Resilience of Coastal Localities: Developing, Implementing, and Sustaining the Use of Coastal Resilience Indicators: A Final Report*, Hazard Reduction and Recovery Center, Texas A&M University, 2010.

18 FEMA, 2019c.

tion against disaster declarations was not statistically significant.[19] We note that in our study, CDRI was the most robust indicator for predicting property damages; it was the only index that performed well across all specifications (per citation, these were "including the use of fixed effects, log-linear and linear specification, negative binomial estimator, and different control variables").

Baseline Resilience Index for Communities

FEMA's National Risk Index uses the Baseline Resilience Index for Communities.[20] The Baseline Resilience Index for Communities assigns community resilience scores at the U.S. county level using data primarily from the year 2000, with some metrics from 2006 and 2007. County maps by state are available for 2010 and 2015. The authors' categorically based method uses publicly available data that can be recalculated over time. The authors' approach is based on a final set of 36 metrics across six categories of resilience: social, economic, institutional, infrastructure, community capital, and environment. The methodology began with a collection of 50 variables that were subjected to correlation and alpha analysis for internal consistency. Highly correlated variables were removed, and the final 36 metrics were retained with an acceptable alpha of 0.7. These variables were then normalized using minimum and maximum to yield the same range between zero and one for each variable. For the final value, metric scores for each category of resilience were averaged and then summed across categories. The Baseline Resilience Index for Communities ranges from 0 (least resilient) to 5 (most resilient), with generally higher resilience in urban and coastal areas. This metric was not empirically validated by its authors, and other tests of validation (against property damages, fatalities, and presidential disaster declarations) failed to find a statistically significant relationship.[21]

Resilience Capacity Index

The Resilience Capacity Index (RCI)[22] assigns community resilience scores to more than 360 U.S. metropolitan areas using data from 2009 to 2010. The authors' categorically based approach evaluates the predisaster resilience level based on 12 metrics across three capacities: regional economic (e.g., economic downturns), sociodemographic, and community connectivity. The 12 metrics were z normalized into scores relative to observed data across all U.S. metropolitan areas, and the final RCI is the average of all 12 scores. Resilience capacity scores range from –1.66 (lowest capacity) to 1.23 (highest capacity). Urban areas across Texas, Alabama, Georgia, southern Florida,

---

[19] Bakkensen et al., 2017.

[20] FEMA, undated a.

[21] Bakkensen et al., 2017.

[22] Bakkensen et al., 2017; K. Foster, "In Search of Regional Resilience," in M. Weir, H. Wial, and H. Wolman, eds., *Building Regional Resilience: Urban and Regional Policy and Its Effects, Vol. 4*, Washington, D.C.: Brookings Institution, 2012.

and the Carolinas show low levels of resilience capacity using RCI. The metric was not empirically validated by its authors, but RCI was compared to employment recovery and GDP data after "a shock." RCI has been shown to be valid in the Gulf Coast region for predicting damages and fatalities; the test of validation against disaster declarations was both insignificant and the incorrect sign.[23]

The Building Code Effectiveness Grading Schedule Program

The Insurance Services Office (ISO) uses the BCEGS program to evaluate how communities enforce local fire and building codes through plan reviews and field inspections. The BCEGS program uses a 1–10 classification scheme to reflect a community's commitment to fire and building code enforcement; 1 signifies exemplary commitment and 10 represents the lowest commitment. Developed in the early 1990s, the BCEGS program incorporated survey responses from more than 7,500 building officials countrywide from the International Conference of Building Officials, the Southern Building Code Congress International, and the Building Officials and Code Administration International. Since its implementation in 1995, the ISO has reviewed more than 15,000 fire and building code departments across the country through the BCEGS program. While FEMA uses the BCEGS program to address urban fire issues, this index could potentially be applied more generally.

Summary of Hazard-Agnostic Metrics

Table 5.1 shows a summary of hazard-agnostic community resilience measures currently thought to be in use at FEMA and discussed above. There are a large number of other potential measures described in both the FEMA-funded November 2019 study and in use at other federal agencies;[24] given the findings of the scorecard test run, we suggest that a broader study could be conducted across many more of these measures (e.g., EPA Climate Resilience Screening Index[25]).

Hazard-Specific Ways to Measure Community Resilience

Hundreds of vulnerability indexes exist (as partially surveyed by the FEMA-sponsored Argonne National Laboratory's report[26]). Here we consider the hazards our method should specifically support and specific metrics that have been developed for those

---

[23] Bakkensen et al., 2017.

[24] FEMA, 2019a.

[25] U.S. Environmental Protection Agency, *Development of a Climate Resilience Screening Index (CRSI): An Assessment of Resilience to Acute Meteorological Events and Selected Natural Hazards*, October 2017.

[26] Lesley Edgemon, Carol Freeman, Carmella Burdi, John Hutchison, Karen Marsh, and Kyle Pfeiffer, *Community Resilience Indicator Analysis: County-Level Analysis of Commonly Used Indicators from Peer-Reviewed Research, 2019 Update*, Washington, D.C.: U.S. Department of Homeland Security, 2019.

Table 5.1
Hazard-Agnostic Community Resilience Measures

Measure	Description	Reference
CRIA	Includes 11 population-focused and 9 community-focused indicators derived from literature review	FEMA, November 2019c.
SoVI	Used by FEMA's National Risk Index and includes 11 socioeconomic vulnerability factors at the U.S. county level	Cutter, Boruff, and Shirley, 2003.
SVI	Assigns social vulnerability scores at the U.S. census-tract level based on 15 socioeconomic variables	Flanagan et al., 2011.
CDRI	Assigns community resilience scores to 144 Gulf State counties based on 75 social, economic, physical, and human indicators	Peacock et al., 2010.
Baseline Resilience Index for Communities	Assigns community resilience scores to U.S. counties based on 36 metrics across social, economic, institutional, infrastructure, community capital, and environment categories	Cutter, Burton, Emrich, 2010.
RCI	Assigns community resilience scores to more than 360 U.S. metropolitan areas based on 12 metrics across regional economic, sociodemographic, and community connectivity capacities	*Berkeley Building Resilient Regions: Resilience Capacity Index*, 2015.
BCEGS	A 1–10 classification scheme to reflect building code enforcement commitment	Jody Dwyer, *The ISO Building Code Effectiveness Grading Schedule*, MTAS Publications: Full Publications, 2012.

hazards. Some of these, such as those in the heat vulnerability category, are indexes. Others, such as FEMA's CRS method, use a checklist approach.

Flood Vulnerability: Community Rating System

Floods are one of the leading causes of deaths and property damages in the country.[27] Through its National Flood Insurance Program (NFIP), FEMA has an existing index used to consider flood vulnerability: the CRS.[28] The CRS is a voluntary FEMA program that offers discounted flood insurance premiums to communities that adopt enhanced techniques for floodplain management. FEMA considers 19 areas for protecting against floods and assigns a community points within these areas for actions taken. The sum of the points indicates the CRS community level, making it an index. The way the points are obtained and summed does not account for synergies in actions.

---

[27] See, for instance, National Weather Service, *Summary of Natural Hazard Statistics for 2017 in the United States*, April 2018.

[28] FEMA, *National Flood Insurance Program Community Rating System Coordinator's Manual*, FEMA FIA-15/2017, Washington, D.C.: FEMA, 2017.

All the items listed in CRS have been (individually) shown to, when enacted, decrease economic losses or deaths during a flood.[29]

In addition, multiple other studies exist that consider flood risks and vulnerability. Some consider general social vulnerability in the context of flood risk and, for example, find that socially vulnerable neighborhoods are prioritized.[30] Others seek to create a flood-specific vulnerability index;[31] in one case, they found that the cost of mitigation was not sensitive to representation of socioeconomic vulnerability.[32] While we note all these other options, we do not include them in our subsequent analysis, because we did not see them currently being used at FEMA.[33]

Hurricane Vulnerability: Institute of Building and Home Safety FORTIFIED Home Program

Hurricanes are one of the leading causes of public assistance spending.[34] Hurricanes induce a variety of natural hazards, such as wind, wind-driven rain, rain, riverine flooding, coastal flooding, tornados, lightning, and sometimes hail/snow. In addition to the flooding-specific discussion listed above, we are aware of multiple programs attempting to increase resilience through improved building codes, such as the Institute of Building and Home Safety (IBHS) FORTIFIED Home Program.[35]

---

[29] For example, Russell Blessing, Samuel D. Brody, and Wesley E. Highfield, "Valuing Floodplain Protection and Avoidance in a Coastal Watershed," *Disasters*, Vol. 43, No. 4, 2019; William Mobley, Kayode O. Atoba, and Wesley E. Highfield, "Uncertainty in Flood Mitigation Practices: Assessing the Economic Benefits of Property Acquisition and Elevation in Flood-Prone Communities," *Sustainability*, Vol. 12, No. 5, 2020, p. 2098.

[30] E. Tate, A. Strong, T. Kraus, and H. Xiong, "Flood Recovery and Property Acquisition in Cedar Rapids, Iowa," *Natural Hazards*, Vol. 80, No. 3, 2016.

[31] For example, A. Fekete, "Validation of a Social Vulnerability Index in Context to River-Floods in Germany," *Natural Hazards and Earth System Science*, Vol. 9, 2009; C. Sebald, *Towards an Integrated Flood Vulnerability Index—a Flood Vulnerability Assessment*, thesis, University of Southampton, 2010; S. Balica, N. Wright, and F. Van Der Meulen, "A Flood Vulnerability Index for Coastal Cities and Its Use in Assessing Climate Change Impacts," *Natural Hazards Review*, Vol. 64, 2012; S. Balica, I. Popescu, L. Beevers, and N. Wright, "Parametric and Physically Based Modelling Techniques for Flood Risk and Vulnerability Assessment: A Comparison," *Environmental Modelling and Software*, Vol. 41, 2013; P. Fernandez, S. Mourato, M. Moreira, and L. Pereira, "A New Approach for Computing a Flood Vulnerability Index Using Cluster Analysis," *Physics and Chemistry of the Earth*, Vol. 94, 2016.

[32] K. Klima, L. El Gammal, W. D. Kong, and D. Prosdocimi, "Creating a Water Risk Index to Improve Community Resilience," *IBM Journal of Research and Development*, Vol. 64, No. 1/2, 2020.

[33] As discussed in Chapter Six below, we suggest that a broader study could be conducted across many more of these measures.

[34] FEMA, "Public Assistance Funded Projects Detail," webpage, undated d; FEMA, "Public Assistance Funded Projects Summary," webpage, undated e.

[35] See, for instance, IBHS, "Disaster Safety," undated.

Wildfire Vulnerability

Wildfires are one of the leading causes of public assistance spending.[36] To our knowledge, all wildfire-specific indexes are similar to CRS in that they are focused on helping a community understand actions they can take to improve resilience. For example, the Firewise USA program encourages community-led efforts to understand and reduce local vulnerability to wildfires.[37] Firewise communities can obtain wildfire risk assessments to guide the creation of risk-reduction action plans that include local volunteering and outreach.

Heat Vulnerability

Generally speaking,[38] measures of heat vulnerability first consider a variety of medical studies suggesting characteristics that increase heat vulnerability and then seek to combine them in some fashion. Commonly mentioned characteristics span social (age, whether one is living alone), economic (poverty levels, education levels, presence of air conditioning, building insulation type), environmental (hyperlocal temperatures, presence of trees or parks), and medical (whether someone has diabetes, heart disease, congestive heart failure, myocardial infarction). Some studies then choose a subset of variables, normalize them on a scale of 0 to 1, and sum them.[39] Other studies seek to characterize a heat vulnerability index.[40] Still other studies obtain actual health data and run regressions attempting to predict deaths as a function of characteristics,[41] thus validating their results. This last set of studies is small in number given the privacy restrictions on health data in the United States.

---

[36] FEMA, undated d; FEMA, undated e.

[37] National Fire Protection Association, "Public Education," webpage, undated.

[38] Heat vulnerability does not typically cause high amounts of property losses, so it has a relatively limited impact on DRF expenditures or the benefit/cost ratios used to evaluate mitigation projects. As such, we did not include heat vulnerability metrics in our subsequent analysis. However, extreme heat is one of the leading causes of fatalities from natural hazards, so we note it here to provide a comprehensive understanding of community resilience.

[39] For example, C. Aubrecht and D. Ozceylan, "Identification of Heat Risk Patterns in the U.S. National Capital Region by Integrating Heat Stress and Related Vulnerability," *Environment International*, Vol. 56, 2013.

[40] For example, K. Bradford, L. Abrahams, M. Hegglin, and K. Klima, "A Heat Vulnerability Index and Adaptation Solutions for Pittsburgh, Pennsylvania," *Environmental Science and Technology*, Vol. 49, No. 19, 2015; C. E. Reid, M. S. O'Neill, C. J. Gronlund, S. J. Brines, D. G. Brown, and A. V. Diez-Roux, "Mapping Community Determinants of Heat Vulnerability," *Environmental Health Perspectives*, Vol. 117, No. 11, 2009; D. M. Hondula, R. E. Davis, M. J. Leisten, M. V. Saha, L. M. Veazey, and C. R. Wegner, "Fine-Scale Spatial Variability of Heat-Related Mortality in Philadelphia County, USA, from 1983–2008: A Case-Series Analysis," *Environmental Health*, Vol. 11, 2012.

[41] For example, Jaime Madrigano, Kazuhiko Ito, Sarah Johnson, Patrick L. Kinney, and Thomas Matte, "A Case-Only Study of Vulnerability to Heat Wave–Related Mortality in New York City (2000–2011)," *Environmental Health Perspectives*, Vol. 123, No. 7, 2015.

Lack of Empirical Validation and Temporal Variations Challenge Existing Indexes

Primary limitations of these indexes include a lack of empirical validation and the fact that they do not include changes in future social vulnerability. Although these indexes are derived from literature and/or subject-matter expertise,[42] they do not validate their assigned vulnerability scores against actual damages.[43] In fact, the resulting index can be largely influenced by the approach used (e.g., inductive versus deductive methods).[44] Consideration and adequate treatment of risk perceptions, coping strategies, and other local risk characteristics are also absent in some of these approaches.[45] Representative issues also exist, because social vulnerability and the characteristics that comprise it change over time. Much like an aging building that becomes more vulnerable to hazards with time, communities experience changes in socioeconomics, land use, and emergency response, as well as in their risk perceptions and ability to cope. To our knowledge, a method for future indexes does not yet exist.

In addition, many of these measures are often created in a way that attempts to separate the vulnerability from the hazard itself (e.g., separate heat vulnerability from extreme heat events). There are some inextricable feedback loops between vulnerability and hazards that will not be captured well by this approach. In addition, there are also temporal considerations (e.g., climate change); this can be partially accounted for by calculating the measure over multiple snapshots of time, but this will certainly be a limitation when considering future events.

Creating the Scorecard

In creating the scorecard, we considered four categories of questions to score potential methods to measure community resilience:

- **Measures Resilience**: Which methods measure community resilience as defined by NIST?

---

[42] For example, C. Giupponi, S. Giove, and V. Giannini, "A Dynamic Assessment Tool for Exploring and Communicating Vulnerability to Floods and Climate Change," *Environmental Modelling and Software*, Vol. 44, 2013; K.-S. Jun, E.-S. Chung, E.-S., Y.-G. Kim, and Y. Kim, "A Fuzzy Multi-Criteria Approach to Flood Risk Vulnerability in South Korea by Considering Climate Change Impacts," *Expert Systems with Applications*, Vol. 40, No. 4, 2013.

[43] For example, B. L. Preston, E. J. Yuen, and R. M. Westaway, "Putting Vulnerability to Climate Change on the Map: A Review of Approaches, Benefits, and Risks," *Sustainability Science*, Vol. 6, No. 2, 2011.

[44] E. Tate, "Social Vulnerability Indices: A Comparative Assessment Using Uncertainty and Sensitivity Analysis," *Natural Hazards*, Vol. 63, No. 2, 2012.

[45] M. B. Soares, A. S. Gagnon, and R. M. Doherty, "Conceptual Elements of Climate Change Vulnerability Assessments: A Review," *International Journal of Climate Change Strategies and Management*, Vol. 4, No. 1, 2012; S. Rufat, E. Tate, C. G. Burton, and A. S. Maroof, "Social Vulnerability to Floods: Review of Case Studies and Implications for Measurement," *International Journal of Disaster Risk Reduction*, Vol. 14, 2015.

- **Addresses Related Stafford Act Compliance**: Which methods (if they worked perfectly) would best address the Stafford criteria?
- **Is Practical and Scientifically Validated**: How well do the methods currently perform across dimensions of validity, reproducibility, and causing no undue burden on the applicant?
- **Measures Things BRIC Grants Can Improve**: Could BRIC project grants directly improve these community resilience scores, and are they generalizable to multiple hazards?

After choosing the categories, we conducted multiple discussions (both internal to the HSOAC team and with the sponsor) to choose high-level merit criteria that fit these four criterion categories. Table 5.2 shows the four criterion categories and ten merit criteria.

Within each of these evaluation criterion categories, we defined merit criteria—a total of ten across the evaluation criterion categories. We defined concepts such that more of a concept would, all other things being equal, likely result in increased community resilience. Then, we created a yes/no rubric for rating community resilience indicators for each of the ten merit criteria. Below, we discuss the evaluation criterion categories and merit criteria in more detail.

Table 5.2
The Ten Merit Criteria for the Four Criterion Categories

Category	Merit Criterion
Measures resilience; corresponds to Stafford Act Section 203g(11)	**Preparation:** Does it measure preparation for anticipated hazards, including predisaster mitigation efforts?
	Adaptability: Does it measure adaptation to changing conditions?
	Recovery: Does it measure ability to withstand/recover rapidly from disruptions?
Closely addresses related Stafford Act criteria	**Section 203(9):** Does it measure small, impoverished community (as defined in law)?
	Section 203(10): Does the metric include whether the community mandates the two most recent building codes and standards and other relevant performance goals?
Is practical and scientifically shown to measure resilience	**Validity:** Has it been shown (in a peer-reviewed, reputable publication) to be correlated with economic losses or deaths?
	Ease of calculation: Could the applicant calculate the measure without possessing significant technical skill?
	No undue burden on applicant: Are data sets publicly available and can calculations be done without specialized software beyond Microsoft Office?
Measures aspects of resilience that a project grant could affect	**Improvable:** Could BRIC projects raise how communities score on the metric?
	Versatile: Can it measure resilience across multiple kinds of hazards?

Measures Resilience

There are 12 criteria that FEMA must consider when awarding BRIC grants. One criterion states: "(11) the extent to which the assistance will fund activities that increase the level of resilience." Clearly, this criterion directly considers resilience. Unfortunately, the legislation does not define what is meant by resilience (nor the relation to community resilience).

Given this, and after discussions with the sponsor, we started with the NIST definition of resilience. This definition had multiple components—related to preparation, adaptability, and recovery, which we broke into three main pieces and which make up the first three merit criteria:

- **Merit Criterion 1: Preparation. Does it measure preparation for anticipated hazards?** This could include whether a hazard mitigation plan exists and the general economic ability of the community (insurance ratings, community budget surplus, bond rating of community, etc.), Community Rating System rating, and so on.
- **Merit Criterion 2: Adaptability. Does it measure adaptation to changing conditions?** This could include the presence and interactiveness of emergency first responders and the general level of social networking/cohesiveness of the community. This, in turn, could mean including ambulance support, hospitals/clinics, nursing homes, and distance to these. This could also reflect those with health-related evacuation requirements, such as those who rely on equipment (e.g., ventilators, wheelchairs) or certain types of medicines (e.g., insulin) or have ambulatory difficulties (e.g., very elderly, those who are bedridden or need wheelchairs).
- **Merit Criterion 3: Recovery. Does it measure the ability to withstand/recover rapidly from disruptions?** This could include considering health (presence of mold, environmental contaminants) and safety (physical safety of the building) of the buildings' users, personal economic indicators not already specifically noted in the "small and impoverished communities" definition (percent of those insured, property prices, per capita income). Communitywide, this includes general welfare topics, such as support of critical lifeline infrastructure (accessibility by transportation after a disaster, support of electricity after a disaster) and availability of industries to begin repairs (e.g., availability of construction industry to begin repairs).

For each of these merit criteria, we defined a "Yes"/"No" rubric. An item would receive a "Yes" if the metric measured any of the items in the rubric description. It would also receive a "Yes" if data used as a key input for the metric satisfied this criterion.

Addresses Related Stafford Act Compliance

We found that two other Stafford Act criteria (Criterion 9 and Criterion 10) relate to the concept of community resilience. We considered each separately, defining merit criteria for each.

The ninth Stafford Act criterion states: "(9) the extent to which assistance will fund mitigation activities in small impoverished communities." The term "small impoverished communities" is defined in legislative authority as

> a community of 3,000 or fewer individuals that is identified by the State as a rural community, and is not a remote area within the corporate boundaries of a larger city; is economically disadvantaged, by having an average per capita annual income of residents not exceeding 80 percent of national, per capita income, based on best available data; the local unemployment rate exceeds by one percentage point or more the most recently reported, average yearly national unemployment rate; and any other factors identified in the State Plan in which the community is located.[46]

The predecessor to BRIC, the PDM program, directly used "small impoverished communities" as one of the decision criteria in its approach. Given this, we used this criterion as is within the rubric. Specifically, the resulting merit criteria is thus:

- **Merit Criterion 4: Does it measure small, impoverished communities (as defined in law)?** The tenth Stafford Act criterion states the following:

> (10) the extent to which the State, local, Indian tribal, or territorial government has facilitated the adoption and enforcement of the latest published editions of relevant consensus-based codes, specifications, and standards, including amendments made by State, local, Indian tribal, or territorial governments during the adoption process that incorporate the latest hazard-resistant designs and establish criteria for the design, construction, and maintenance of residential structures and facilities that may be eligible for assistance under this chapter for the purpose of protecting the health, safety, and general welfare of the buildings' users against disasters.[47]

This criterion has two pieces that appear to be relevant to community resilience. First, consider the phrase "relevant consensus-based codes, specifications, and standard." Per law, this means "with respect to relevant consensus-based codes, specifications, and standards, the 2 most recently published editions."[48] For example, note that the 2018 interim Natural Hazard Mitigation Saves report uses the 2015 and 2018

[46] 42 U.S.C. 5133.

[47] 42 U.S.C. 5133.

[48] 42 U.S.C. 5133.

International Residential Code and International Building Code in its analysis.[49] Note that this covers solely whether codes are adopted; the Stafford Act does not include a measure of enforcement. Thus, we limit this merit criterion to adoption.

Next, consider that FEMA has stated in an online glossary that "[b]uilding codes protect public health, safety, and general welfare as they relate to construction and occupancy of buildings and structures."[50] This suggests that beyond the existence of building codes, we think this also relates to identifying performance goals based on community needs and the social systems where they operate. This could mean allowing for the consideration of community-specific items, such as buildings, monuments, and areas of special meaning. The resulting merit criterion is thus:

- **Merit Criterion 5: Does the metric include whether the community mandates the two most recent building codes and standards *and* other relevant performance goals?** As we did for each of these merit criteria, we defined a "Yes"/"No" rubric. An item would receive a "Yes" if the metric measured any of the items in the rubric description or if a key data input for the metric satisfied that criterion.

Is Practical and Scientifically Validated

Informal discussions with the sponsor have suggested that FEMA is interested in methods that are valid and reproducible and do not place undue burden on the applicant. Given this, we included these as three separate merit criteria:

- **Merit Criterion 6: Validity. Has it been shown (in a peer-reviewed, reputable publication) to be correlated with economic losses or deaths?** This receives a "Yes" if the measure has been demonstrated in the peer-reviewed/reputable literature to be valid for at least a few locations in the United States.[51]
- **Merit Criterion 7: Ease of Calculation. Could the applicant calculate the measure without possessing significant technical skill?** This receives a "Yes" if calculations are relatively easy; two reasonably trained people (e.g., high school graduates, undergraduate students) would be reasonably expected to get the same answer.
- **Merit Criterion 8: No Undue Burden on Applicant. Are data sets publicly available, and can calculations be done without specialized software beyond**

---

[49] Multihazard Mitigation Council, *Natural Hazard Mitigation Saves: 2018 Interim Report*, principal investigator K. Porter; co–principal investigators C. Scawthorn and C. Huyck; investigators: R. Eguchi, Z. Hu, A. Reeder, and P. Schneider, director, Washington, D.C.: National Institute of Building Sciences, 2018.

[50] FEMA, "Glossary," webpage, undated b.

[51] Metrics that do well on predicting population level impacts will not necessarily do well on predicting economic impacts. If the goal is to predict direct economic impacts, it is fairly easy to predict that based on population and wealth. If you want indirect economic impacts, one needs to look at the structure of the economy.

Microsoft Office? This receives a "Yes" if data sets are publicly available and calculation does not require additional software beyond Microsoft Office.

Measures Things That the Building Resilient Infrastructure and Community Program's Grants Can Improve

Finally, since it is not quite clear what the federal government means by community resilience, there are a number of different "flavors" (as described in the body of the report). Some of these are types of community resilience metrics that BRIC grants could be structured to improve, whereas others are not. For instance, a BRIC grant cannot really do much about the demographics (age, ethnicity, education levels, etc.) of a region. Conversely, a BRIC grant could greatly affect presence and adherence to a hazard mitigation plan. After speaking with the sponsor, we broke this into two merit criteria:

- **Merit Criterion 9: Improvable. Could BRIC projects raise how communities score on the metric?** The answer would be "Yes" if more than 75 percent of the data informing this community resilience approach can be affected by a BRIC grant over a short project lifetime (e.g., one year).
- **Merit Criterion 10: Versatile. Can it measure resilience across multiple kinds of hazards?** This is very simple to answer; "Yes" if this is either hazard-agnostic or includes consideration of all major hazards, and "No" if it is hazard-specific.

The resulting scorecard that uses the four sets of criteria from Table 5.2 is shown in Figure 5.1. We note this is a suggested scorecard; FEMA may wish to use other merit criteria or alter the methods of grouping evaluation criteria (where some are a "must include all" and others are a "must include at least one"). For example, FEMA may prefer that instead of measuring only one part of resilience, all three merit criteria must be included. Indeed, one might argue that to best support community resilience, a metric must measure as many parts of the NIST definition as possible.

Assuming FEMA decisionmakers would like to tailor the decision criteria, the scoring criteria and scorecard should be updated.

Community Resilience Metric Assessment Test-Run Results

Based on input from two HSOAC SMEs, we conducted a test run of the scorecard. Specifically, the two SMEs rated ten separate measures for the ten merit criteria.

To help illustrate the thought process behind interpreting the rubric, the two SMEs came to agreement and provided the filled-out worked scorecard for CRS (Figure 5.2). For each of the ten merit criteria, we use the extended rubric above to answer "Yes" or "No" to the questions shown in Figure 5.1:

Figure 5.1
Blank Scorecard

Name:	**Rating Yes/No**	**Total Yeses**
Evaluation Criterion 1: Measures Resilience		
1. Measures preparation for future hazards?		Discard if all are "No"
2. Measures adaptability to change?		
3. Measures ability to withstand/recover?		
Evaluation Criterion 2: Addresses Related Stafford Act Compliance		
4. Measures small, impoverished communities?		"Yes" are extra credit
5. Measures building code adoption?		
Evaluation Criteria on: Is Practical and Scientifically Validated		
6. Shown to correlate with loss or mortality?		Discard if any are "No"
7. Easy to calculate without major expertise?		
8. Calculable without specialized resources?		
Evaluation Criteria on: Measures Things BRIC Grants Can Improve		
9. Could BRIC project grants improve how community scores on this metric?		Discard if any are "No"
10. Measures resilience for most hazards?		

- We answer "Yes" to Merit Criterion 1 because the metric includes the measurement of the presence of a floodplain management plan, which demonstrates preparation for a future hazard.
- We answer "Yes" to Merit Criterion 2 because the metric includes the measurement of attempts to improve emergency preparedness and response; per the rubric definition, this shows adaptability to change.
- We answer "Yes" to Merit Criterion 3 because most of the measurements within the CRS criteria are structured to improve a community's ability to withstand hazards.
- We answer "No" to Merit Criterion 4 because the measurement does not include small and impoverished communities.
- We answer "Yes" to Merit Criterion 5 because the adoption of building codes is in CRS. Note, we are assuming because of the language that the adoption of these codes means that they align with the two most recent building codes
- We answer "Yes" to Merit Criterion 6 because all the items listed in CRS have been (individually) shown to, when enacted, decrease economic losses or deaths

Figure 5.2
Scorecard Test Run—Community Rating System

Name: Community Rating System	Rating Yes/No	Total Yeses
Evaluation Criterion 1: Measures Resilience		✓
1. Measures preparation for future hazards?	Yes	3 yeses—keep
2. Measures adaptability to change?	Yes	
3. Measures ability to withstand/recover?	Yes	
Evaluation Criterion 2: Addresses Related Stafford Act Compliance		✓
4. Measures small, impoverished community?	No	One extra credit yes
5. Measures building code existence?	Yes	
Evaluation Criterion 3: Is Practical and Scientifically Validated		✓
6. Shown to correlate with loss/mortality?	Yes	3 yeses—keep
7. Easy to calculate without major expertise?	Yes	
8. Calculable without specialized resources?	Yes	
Evaluation Criterion 4: Measures Things BRIC Grants Can Improve		X
9. Could BRIC project grants improve how community scores on this metric?	Yes	Fails last test
10. Measures resilience for most hazards?	No	

NOTE: A checkmark (✓) indicates that the metric passes that evaluation criterion. An **X** indicates that the metric did not pass.

during a flood.[52] We note that we are not aware of a study looking at the full set of combinations of items within CRS.

- We answer "Yes" to Merit Criterion 7 because the metric is calculated by the federal government at regular intervals; thus, the stakeholder does not need to make a calculation.
- We answer "Yes" to Merit Criterion 8 because the ratings are freely available online at FEMA; thus, no additional software is needed to get the rating.
- We answer "Yes" to Merit Criterion 9 because many of the items in the metric are items that have been directly affected by other FEMA grants in the past (e.g., elevation of a house or a planning grant to make a hazard mitigation plan). Specifically, CRS includes 19 different criteria across four bins of (1) improving public information (seven items), (2) mapping and regulations (five items), (3) flood

---

[52] For example, Blessing, Brody, and Highfield, 2019; Mobley, Atoba, and Highfield, 2020.

damage reduction (four items), and (4) flood preparedness (three items).[53] We think planning or mitigation grants have supported all of (1), (2), and (3) but that all of (4) are not currently addressed by BRIC grants.

- We answer "No" to Merit Criterion 10 because CRS is, by design, constructed to be flood specific.

Figure 5.3 shows full test-run rankings for all the metrics to measure community resilience based on two HSOAC SMEs. Our preliminary rating by two HSOAC SMEs suggests that no single metric meets all criteria. However, given this is only a test run and that only two raters were involved, it is important for FEMA to assemble a large group of SMEs to customize and improve definitions of yes/no and collect a broader range of potential measures and conduct their own ranking before considering any findings "final."

In this test run of the framework, the two HSOAC SMEs found that the framework was practical and able to provide useful insights on the relative merits of each measure. Their assessments are not sufficient to truly evaluate the measure—that would require many FEMA SMEs using and improving the framework. However, we offer some basic insights from their test run that may help FEMA SMEs think about how to evaluate measures and where to start in taking stock of the measures already in use within the organization.

First, we note that resilience metrics do not all measure comparable concepts. Many resilience metrics focus on difficult-to-change characteristics of populations that place a community at an advantage/disadvantage in attempting to be resilient to natural hazards. These metrics can be focused on vulnerability (disadvantage) and/or resiliency resources (advantage). Other metrics focus on actions that communities can take to diminish future losses. These metrics can be focused on preparedness and/or mitigation. In general, resiliency measures tend to rely heavily on census data, which bias measurement toward difficult-to-change population characteristics. However, a program like BRIC may benefit more from metrics that focus on actions that communities can take to diminish future losses because (1) BRIC grants can specifically fund some of these actions and (2) BRIC grant performance can be evaluated in terms of whether more of these actions are taken in grant-recipient communities. No BRIC grant can make old people young (a common item in vulnerability indexes), but BRIC grants can fund tornado safe rooms (a mitigation measure) that will increase their chances of surviving a natural hazard. FEMA NFIP's CRS is an example of a measure that is based on mitigation action.

Second, we note that vulnerability measures may be particularly well suited to measuring equity gaps in program outcomes. These outcomes might include applica-

[53] FEMA, *National Flood Insurance Program Community Rating System: A Local Official's Guide to Saving Lives, Preventing Property Damage, and Reducing the Cost of Flood Insurance*, Washington, D.C.: FEMA, 2018.

Figure 5.3
Full Rankings for Metric to Measure Community Resilience

	Metric to Measure Community Resilience									
Evaluation Criterion	Argonne	SoVI	SVI	CDRI	BRIC	RCI	CRS	IBHS	BCEGS	Firewise
Evaluation Criterion 1: Measures Resilience	✓	✓	✓	✓	✓	✓	✓	✓	✓	✓
1. Measures preparation for future hazards?	N	Y	N	Y	Y	N	Y	Y	Y	N
2. Measures adaptability to change?	Y	Y	Y	Y	Y	Y	Y	N	N	N
3. Measures ability to withstand/recover?	Y	Y	Y	Y	Y	N	Y	Y	Y	N
Evaluation Criterion 2: Stafford Act Compliance	~	~	~	✓	~	~	✓	✓	✓	~
4. Measures small, impoverished communities?	N	N	N	N	N	N	N	N	N	N
5. Measures building code existence?	N	N	N	Y	N	N	Y	Y	Y	N
Evaluation Criterion 3: Practical and Validated	X	X	✓	X	X	X	✓	X	X	X
6. Shown to correlate with loss (L) or mortality (M)?	N	N	Y (L, M)	Y (L, M)	N	Y (L, M)	Y (L)	Y (L)	Y (L)	N
7. Easy to calculate without major expertise?	Y	N	Y	N	N	N	Y	N	N	N
8. Calculable without specialized resources?	Y	Y	Y	N	Y	Y	Y	N	N	N
Evaluation Criterion 4: BRIC Project Impact	X	X	X	X	X	X	X	X	X	X
9. Could BRIC project grants improve how community scores on this metric?	N	N	N	N	N	N	Y	N	N	N
10. Measures resilience for most hazards?	Y	Y	Y	Y	Y	Y	N	N	Y	N

NOTE: In this table, a Y/N indicates that a metric does/does not meet each of the ten merit criteria. In addition, the merit criteria are grouped into evaluation criteria. A ✓/X indicates that the metric passes/does not pass that evaluation criterion. Unique to evaluation criterion 2, which consists of merit criteria that are nice but not necessary, is a ~: This symbol indicates that while none of the merit criteria were met, the metric technically still passes the evaluation criteria. Shading denotes the three metrics that are the top scoring metrics. Note, for "Shown to correlate with loss," we used (as described in the rubric) the existence of a peer-reviewed study. For SVI, CDRI, and RCI, note that the validation study of Bakkensen et al., 2017, shows, surprisingly, that the metrics are useful for predicting both damages (in the form of economic losses) and fatalities.

tions won per applications submitted, projects completed on budget per projects completed, or even average cost to applicant per application submitted. For each of these outcomes, one could measure the size of the gap between the average vulnerable community applicant and the average nonvulnerable community applicant. This could be broken down by subcomponents of the vulnerability measure, and targeted strategies could be formulated for closing the gap over successive years. CDC's SVI is an example of a vulnerability measure that can easily be broken down into component measures and used for equity gap measurement.

Third, we note that building codes are frequently emphasized in the revised Stafford Act Section 203 but often underrepresented in resilience measures. This may reflect the lack of census-based measures of code resilience, the highly detailed nature of building codes, or the discrepancy between code adoption and code enforcement. If FEMA selects resilience measures that do not include a code adoption/enforcement component, it may be necessary to augment that measure for a building-code-specific measure. BCEGS is an example of a multihazard building code quality measure that provides visibility on both codes adopted and ongoing code enforcement.

Summary

According to the NIST definition, "community resilience is the ability to prepare for anticipated hazards, adapt to changing conditions, and withstand and recovery rapidly from disruptions." We conducted a review of community resilience measures thought to be in use at FEMA, profiling ten measures of resilience, vulnerability, and/or building code quality. We then created an evaluation assessment scorecard that FEMA SMEs can use to determine what community resilience measures are best suited to support the needs of the BRIC program, focusing on four factors: (1) ability to measure key aspects of the NIST community resilience concept; (2) ability to measure Stafford Act compliance with related concepts; (3) practicality, including scientific validations work conducted to date; and (4) ability to meet BRIC-specific needs for a hazard-neutral measure that BRIC grants can plausibly affect. Two HSOAC SMEs conducted a test run of the evaluation framework on ten measures, finding it both useful and able to provide insight.

While we provide no recommendations for a specific measure, we do note three general insights from their evaluation exercise. First, measures that focus on actions that communities can take may be more useful to BRIC than measures that focus on difficult-to-change census population characteristics. FEMA NFIP's CRS is an example of an action-based measure. Second, vulnerability measures based on difficult-to-change census population characteristics may be better suited to the measurement of equity gaps in program outcomes, especially if they can easily be decomposed into component measures to provide more detailed insights. CDC's SVI is an example of a census-based vulnerability measure that can be easily decomposed into straightforward components. Third, building codes are heavily emphasized in the revised Stafford Act Section 203 but are often missing from resilience measures—especially census-based measures. Most options for measuring resilience may need to be augmented with a building code adoption/enforcement measure to improve statutory compliance. ISO's BCEGS is an example of a building code adoption and enforcement quality measure.

CHAPTER SIX

Conclusions and Recommendations

Conclusions

This project developed metrics to support decisionmaking for FEMA's BRIC predisaster mitigation program. Building from discussions with program leadership, a review of stakeholder comments, and a close reading of BRIC's legal requirements, we established three LoEs. The **indirect benefits line** reviewed published measurement techniques and blended them into instructions for an I-O simulation model that better measures the true benefit to a community of mitigating an asset. The **AIC line** reviewed a sample of analogous research and interviewed SMEs to develop a checklist for assessing the ability of applicants to propose/execute mitigation projects. The **community resilience line** developed an assessment framework based on BRIC's legal requirements, discussions with BRIC leadership, and standard best practices in measurement. Then, the LoE conducted a preliminary review of published resilience metrics using the assessment framework. As shown in Table 6.1, each LoE produced a metric or framework for assessing metrics that could support BRIC grant decisionmaking and program performance evaluation.

Recommendations

In this section, we provide recommendations based on the findings of the three LoEs contained in Chapters Three, Four, and Five. In each case, we offer the recommendation, along with the rationale for it. We start with one overarching recommendation.

Overarching Recommendation

Recommendation 1: Develop a Strategy for Addressing Known Disaster Relief Fund Cost Drivers

The Stafford Act requires predisaster mitigation programs to be cost-effective. If cost-effectiveness is defined as having the program cost less than the DRF assistance funding the program strives to prevent, having a specific strategy for addressing the DRF's primary cost drivers will improve the program's cost-effectiveness. As discussed in the

Table 6.1
Examples of How Line-of-Effort Products Can Support the Building Resilient Infrastructure and Community Program

LoE	Indirect Benefits	AIC	Community Resilience
Decisionmaking support	Consider a project more desirable if it averts more economic loss across the community.	Provide a customized technical support package to an applicant, based on AIC risk factors.	Use assessment framework to choose a high-quality community resilience measure that is well suited to measuring the resilience impact of BRIC grants. For the metric selected: Consider a project as more valuable if it will improve the community resilience score of the community.
Cost-effectiveness performance evaluation	Establish targets for total economic damage averted across each year's portfolio of BRIC awards.	Measure the gap between high- and low-capability applicants in terms of proposal quality and on-time/on-budget project execution. Establish annual targets for shrinking gap, eventually closing it entirely.	Use assessment framework to choose a high-quality community resilience measure that is well suited to measuring the resilience impact of BRIC grants. For the metric selected: Set targets for average increase in resilience because of BRIC projects.
Equity performance evaluation	Automate I-O modeling to the extent that there is no difference in I-O use between high- and low-capability applicants.	Measure the gap between high- and low-capability applicants in terms of application win/loss rates. Establish annual targets for shrinking the gap, eventually closing it entirely.	Use assessment framework to choose a high-quality community resilience measure that is well suited to measuring the resilience impact of BRIC grants. For the metric selected: Analyze community resilience scores for low-capacity jurisdictions to find opportunities where a well-targeted project will significantly improve resilience, and proactively propose it to the potential applicant.
Contribution to Stafford Act compliance	Section 203g(8): provides visibility on "net benefit to society."	Section 203g(9): provides visibility on the disadvantages that "small, impoverished communities" may face.	Section 203g(11): provides visibility on "community resilience."

NOTE: Not every project needs to contribute to every performance objective. By setting performance objectives at the project portfolio level, different ensembles of projects can be funded strategically to ensure that improvement is made toward all objectives.

Scope section of Chapter One and Appendix A, there are multiple reasons why the past may be a poor guide to the future. If the past does offer some lessons for the future, Appendix A suggests that past DRF IA/PA assistance costs are heavily outlier driven.

Developing specific cost-control strategies for outlier disaster sizes, disaster types, geographic areas, and built structure types may enable BRIC to increase DRF cost savings.

Indirect Benefits Line of Effort

Recommendation 2: In Near-Term, Use a Tailored Input-Output Model to Measure Communitywide Indirect Benefits of Mitigation Projects

Communities are systems, consisting of many interdependent elements. When a disaster occurs, elements may incur direct damage but may also be disrupted because of damage to other elements on which they depend. Averting this disruption is the indirect benefit of a mitigation project. Measuring indirect benefit improves visibility on the full range the benefits and costs of a mitigation project. It also provides insight on how a mitigated asset might improve community resilience. I-O models use data on economic interdependence to understand how disruptions might propagate outward as changes in the flow of goods and services. Comparing simulation runs with the mitigation project to one without such a mitigation project, I-O models can quantify this disruption in terms of total drop in economic output. Combining an empirically grounded understanding of community interdependence with a straightforward way to value disruptions, I-O models are a strong candidate for measuring the indirect benefits of a mitigation project.

However, what really sets I-O models apart is ease of use. First, the model generalizes easily to different communities at different scales—just swap in the correct I-O table for that geography. Second, the model relies on widely available data, either from commercial sources or free public sources. Third, the model relies on a straightforward matrix multiplication process and, thus, requires less technical expertise than its alternatives. Fourth, while I-O models were not originally designed for disaster modeling, various technical improvements have been developed that can enable them to model the disaster recovery content more faithfully. One such improvement involves utilizing estimates of sector resilience—the ability of industries to moderate the realized impacts of a disruption through adaptation. While various estimates of sector resilience exist in the literature, they are somewhat sensitive to the context in which they were estimated. For this reason, we recommend conducting additional studies to calculate sector resilience coefficients for a range of relevant disaster scenarios that can then be incorporated into an I-O model. Chapter Three describes the findings contributing to this recommendation in more detail. Appendix B details the exact strategy we recommend, with detailed instructions and examples.

Recommendation 3: Integrate the Indirect Benefits Model into Hazus and Automate as Much as Possible

Chapter Four suggests that staff quality—training, experience, and skill—strongly impact an applicant's ability to propose and execute mitigation projects. Under these circumstances, taking steps to minimize the skill needed to develop a project proposal may make the competition fairer among differently resourced applicants and give high-benefit projects in low-skill applicant jurisdictions a better chance of being recognized. As detailed in Chapter Three, we found that I-O modeling could be automated and integrated into Hazus. Hazus provides projections that would supply the initial disruption inputs for the I-O model, which could then draw on a repository of downloaded BEA data to determine the communitywide indirect benefits of mitigating that disruption. In addition, this same modeling approach could theoretically be used to suggest potential projects to applicants.

Recommendation 4: Decide Whether a Computable General Equilibrium Model or Input-Output Model Best Suits the Long-Term Needs of the Building Resilient Infrastructure and Community Program

In Chapter Three, we find that all options for modeling indirect benefits make aggressive assumptions and can only achieve accuracy at the level of broad approximation. However, we identify I-O and CGE as the two best alternatives for modeling indirect benefits. I-O models are easier to use, require less applicant expertise, provide more consistency across geographies, and provide a serviceable approximation of how disasters affect economies in the short term. CGE models require more applicant expertise and generalize less well across different geographies. However, they are better able to model the patterns of adaptation that may occur as households and companies cope with postdisaster economies in the long term. This becomes particularly important for large-scale disasters, which may involve months or even years of recovery. Compared to CGE, I-O models may overestimate the indirect benefits of mitigation for these large-scale disasters because the I-O framework provides less sophisticated tools for modeling adaptation.

While we recommend I-O in the short term (Recommendation 2), we recognize that FEMA may wish to switch over to a CGE approach in the long term to have more detailed projections of long-term adaptation. For this reason, we have included specifications for building the I-O model and CGE model to be as interchangeable as possible—accepting similar inputs and generating similar outputs—in Appendix B. However, FEMA will need to decide whether the downsides of the CGE approach are worth its potential advantages or the I-O approach is the best option in the long term.

Applicant Institutional Capacity Line of Effort

Recommendation 5: Evaluate Applicant Capability to Propose/Execute High-Quality Mitigation Projects and Develop Strategies for Supporting Lower-Capability Applicants

In investigating AIC, our interviewees unanimously confirmed that applicants vary widely in capability and that less-capable applicants were less able to propose/execute mitigation projects successfully. Our respondents were often quick to point out that many factors are outside any applicant's control—disaster disruptions, weather, funding disbursement delays—but also consistently noted that less-resourced applicants were at a disadvantage compared to better-resourced applicants. It is likely that at least some high-benefit mitigation projects do not come to FEMA's attention because they are under the jurisdiction of less-resourced applicants. Taking steps to identify and support lower-capability applicants may make BRIC outcomes more equitable and ensure that high-benefit projects in less-resourced jurisdictions come to the attention of BRIC decisionmakers.

Recommendation 6: In Evaluating Applicant Capability, Focus on Staff Retention, Staff Skill and Experience, Management Capability, and Technical Capability

As detailed in Chapter Four, there was wide agreement that access to and effective management of high-quality staff was the most important factor distinguishing high-capacity applicants from low-capacity ones. Figure 4.1 reports 12 specific items that BRIC decisionmakers can use to evaluate applicant capability. Information on these items can be assessed through the application process and used to provide support for low-capability applicants. Examples of that support might include providing the following:

- a voluntary separate competition "lane" that funds lower-stakes projects but provides a higher level of technical support throughout the project. (Design this lane to improve AIC through experience building and education. Give lane "graduates" priority in the main BRIC application progress for the first few years after graduation.)
- feedback on how to improve capacity
- access to training
- recommendations for implementing relevant management standard operating procedures, perhaps even boilerplate policy text
- support for some form of resource pooling across multiple low-capacity jurisdictions.

Community Resilience Line of Effort

Recommendation 7: Periodically Assess Community Resilience Measures and Encourage Usage at the Federal Emergency Management Agency of Measures That Performed Well on the Assessment

Table 5.1 documents a small selection of the many community resilience measures available, focusing on measures in use at FEMA. Researchers are likely to continue creating community resilience measures, and FEMA's community resilience needs are likely to evolve over time. Periodically assessing available measures and updating the assessment standards can synchronize measure use across FEMA and encourage reliance on high-quality measures. It could even lead to building organizational consensus for using a common indicator or set of indicators. Figure 5.1 provides an initial assessment framework that FEMA SMEs can use, as well as our preliminary findings from demonstrating the use of the framework on a range of measures.

Recommendation 8: In Evaluating Community Resilience, Focus on Resilience (National Institute of Standards and Technology Definition), Stafford Act Compliance, Scientific Validation, and Practicality

As itemized in Table 5.2, there are multiple priorities to consider when evaluating community resilience measures. First, does it measure resilience? Assessing how well it measures the three parts of NIST's resilience definition—preparation for disasters, adaptability to changing conditions, and rapid recovery from disasters—answers this question. Second, does it measure important related concepts? Assessing how well it measures criteria from Section 203 of the Stafford Act answers this question. We focus on Sections 203g(9) and 203g(10), but Table 2.1 provides a complete list of criteria. Third, is the measure valid and practical? Assessing whether peer-reviewed scientific validation studies have been published and whether an applicant could easily obtain scores addresses this question. Fourth, can FEMA assistance—especially BRIC grants—affect the scores? This is important because it determines whether the community resilience (to all hazards) scores can be used as performance indicators. We recommend that the relevant decisionmakers at FEMA update the draft scorecard to best reflect their priorities. Then, we suggest using a larger sample size of SMEs (five to ten, at least) to rate many more measures than are considered here (perhaps all the measures in both this report and other published FEMA literature reviews). This should help improve both the decision aid and the quality of the decision reached.

Recommendation 9: Use Action-Based Community Resilience Metrics to Evaluate Performance

Many measures of community resilience use census data and focus on difficult-to-change population attributes. This measurement strategy may be ill suited for BRIC because it makes it difficult to measure the impact of BRIC grants on community resilience. For example, no BRIC grant could possibly be expected to make old people young, and census data on local elderly populations are often used as an indicator of less resilient communities. In contrast, some metrics focus on actions that communities can take to improve resilience through predisaster preparation and mitigation. These metrics measure a community against the steps it could be taking to be as resilient as possible and enable BRIC to measure whether its grants are moving the community closer to that state. FEMA NFIP's CRS is an example of an action-based metric that has been scientifically validated to correlate with future losses avoided. While CRS is specific to one hazard (flooding), the measurement strategy underlying CRS could theoretically be generalized to an all-hazards metric.

Recommendation 10: Consider Population-Based Community Resilience Metrics to Evaluate Equity Gaps

As noted above, many measures of community resilience use census data and focus on difficult-to-change population attributes. A subset of those measures focuses on vulnerability—population attributes that correspond to societal disadvantages that may reduce community resilience. Such measures may be useful for measuring equity gaps in program outcomes and determining strategies for closing those gaps. For example, one measure of program equity outcomes might be the percentage of successful applications as a fraction of all applications submitted (the application "win rate"). One could use a vulnerability measure to determine whether societally disadvantaged applicants have a lower win-rate and which component of the measure most closely corresponds to that gap and then devise strategies for closing the equity gap. CDC's SVI is an example of a scientifically validated vulnerability measure that can easily be split into component measures.

Recommendation 11: Consider Building Code Adoption/Enforcement Metrics to Improve Statutory Compliance If Not Already Part of the Community Resilience Metric Chosen

The revised Stafford Act Section 203 emphasizes the importance of building codes. However, many resilience measures do not include building code quality and enforcement, perhaps because of the difficulty of quantifying differences in these voluminous, detailed texts. If FEMA SMEs do not select community resilience metrics that include building codes, adopting a specific metric will improve Stafford Act compliance. ISO's BCEGS is an example of a building code quality and enforcement metric.

APPENDIX A

Analysis of Disaster Relief Fund Public and Individual Assistance Costs

Mitigation funds come from DRF, which finances FEMA's assistance activities following a declared disaster.[1] The Stafford Act requires that mitigation programs be cost-effective,[2] meaning that the cost of the predisaster mitigation project is less than the postdisaster response/recovery cost that it is designed to prevent.[3] This appendix examines the historical costs of assistance provided after a declared disaster, drawing out some of the implications for mitigation program policy.

Methods

To conduct this analysis, we downloaded three files from the OpenFEMA data portal:[4]

- Disaster Declaration Summaries is a data set of all federal declared disasters. We used this data set to develop a roster of all disaster declarations, the type of incident declared, and the fiscal year in which it was declared.
- Registration Intake and Individuals Household Program provides statistics on IA activities. We used this data set to determine the IA costs to DRF from each disaster in each county or county-equivalent.
- Public Assistance Funded Projects Detailed provides statistics on PA activities. We used this data set to determine the PA costs to DRF from each disaster in each county or county-equivalent.

[1] Robert T. Stafford Disaster Relief and Emergency Assistance Act, Section 203i(1).

[2] Robert T. Stafford Disaster Relief and Emergency Assistance Act, Section 203e(1)(A).

[3] FEMA, *E/L 0276 Benefit-Cost Analysis Training Student Manual*, Washington, D.C.: FEMA, June 2019a.

[4] FEMA, "OpenFEMA Data Repository," webpage, last updated October 15, 2018.

We merged these files into a composite data set, used the consumer price index[5] to adjust all costs to be 2019 dollars, and matched county-equivalents to metro areas (Census Bureau core-based statistical areas). In total, we were able to merge data for 1,974 declarations over the 2004–2019 period out of the 1,993 declarations in the Disaster Declaration Summaries file. In 2019 dollars, these 1,974 declarations describe a total of $59.4 billion in PA projects and $15.1 billion in IA projects.

Findings

Table A.1 displays the DRF PA and DRF IA costs for the ten most costly disasters in the 2004–2019 period. This table shows that unusually costly disasters ("Outliers") are responsible for the majority of PA/IA disaster assistance costs. The ten events account for about two-thirds of all costs. The top three events—Hurricanes Katrina, Sandy, and Maria—account for 53 percent alone. Also noteworthy is the prevalence of tropical cyclones. Not every tropical cyclone is an outlier, but outliers often tend to be tropical cyclones. Because Katrina, Sandy, and Maria are so disproportionally expensive, we have treated them as outliers and dropped them from the totals in all subsequent tables.

Table A.1
Public Assistance/Individual Assistance Expenditures for the Ten Most Expensive Disasters, 2004–2019

Disaster	Total PA + IA Costs, as a Percentage	Total Costs, in Billions of Dollars		
		PA + IA	PA	IA
2005 tropical cyclone (La., Miss., Fla., Ala.)	32	**49.4**	40.6	8.7
2012 tropical cyclone (13 declarations)	14	**21.3**	19.7	1.6
2017 tropical cyclone (P.R., V.I.)	7	**10.5**	9.1	1.3
2008 tropical cyclone (Tex.)	3	**4.4**	3.7	0.6
2017 tropical cyclone (Tex)	2	**3.9**	2.2	1.7
2006 tropical cyclone (Fla.)	2	**3.7**	3.3	0.4
2017 tropical cyclone (V.I., P.R., Fla., Ga.)	2	**3.3**	2.2	1.1
2008 severe storm (Iowa)	2	**2.8**	2.6	0.2
2005 tropical cyclone (La.)	1	**2.1**	1.4	0.7
2004 tropical cyclone (Fla.)	1	**2**	1.4	0.6

NOTE: Costs are in billions of 2019 dollars.

[5] U.S. Bureau of Labor Statistics, "Consumer Price Index," webpage, undated.

Table A.2 enumerates the total IA and PA for four-year periods between 2004 and 2019. The data suggest that spending can vary widely from period to period. However, 72–86 percent of expenditures resulted from PA spending, indicating that PA drives total costs much more than IA. Within PA, 39–58 percent of funds consist of temporary activity to remediate the immediate aftermath of a disaster—debris removal and emergency protective measures. Among work designed to produce permanent remediations, about equal funding went toward roads/bridges, public buildings, and public utilities—about 29–49 percent of all PA funds and 69–81 percent of all permanent work funds. Within IA, housing assistance accounts for the majority of costs—60 to 89 percent. Much of this is repair work for owner-occupied houses.

Tropical cyclones caused the most PA/IA costs of any type of disaster across all four periods (Table A.3). Excluding the three outliers—Katrina, Sandy, and Maria—tropical cyclones or severe storms alternated as the most-costly type of disaster and were responsible for a combined 58–96 percent of all costs. Just four types of incidents—

Table A.2
Total Costs by Program Category for Declared Disasters, 2004–2019

Program Category	2004–2007	2008–2011	2012–2015	2016–2019
Total costs	**24.7**	**25.3**	**6.5**	**18.1**
Total PA costs	19.5	21.3	5.6	13.1
Total IA costs	5.2	4.0	0.9	5.0
PA emergency work	**9.8**	**8.4**	**2.4**	**7.6**
Debris removal (Category A)	5.3	3.2	1.3	3.7
Emergency protective measures (Category B)	4.5	5.2	1.1	3.9
PA permanent work	**9.2**	**12.1**	**3.1**	**4.9**
Roads and bridges (Category C)	2.1	2.8	1.4	1.4
Water control facilities (Category D)	0.5	0.5	0.2	0.4
Public buildings and contents (Category E)	2.7	3.7	0.5	1.2
Public utilities (Category F)	2.6	3.9	0.6	1.2
Parks and recreational (Category G)	1.3	1.2	0.4	0.7
Management costs (Category Z)	0.4	0.8	0.2	0.5
IA	**5.2**	**3.9**	**1.0**	**5.0**
Housing assistance	3.1	3.3	0.8	3.8
Other needs assistance	2.1	0.6	0.2	1.2

NOTE: Costs are in billions of 2019 dollars; excludes Hurricanes Katrina, Sandy, and Maria.

Table A.3
Total Costs by Disaster Category for Declared Disasters, 2004–2019

Disaster Category	2004–2007	2008–2011	2012–2015	2016–2019
Tropical cyclone	16.9	8.9	0.9	10.6
Severe storm(s)	6.8	12	2.8	1.4
Flood	0	1.8	1.6	4.1
Fire	0.3	0.8	0.4	1.5
Severe ice storm	0.2	0.8	0.4	0
Snow	0.3	0.5	0	0.3
Earthquake	0.1	0.2	0.1	0
Tornado	0	0.2	0.1	0.1
Other	0.1	0.1	0.1	0.1

NOTE: Costs are in billions of 2019 dollars; excludes Hurricanes Katrina, Sandy, and Maria.

tropical cyclones, severe storms, floods, and fires—were responsible for 90–97 percent of costs in any given period.

While urban areas[6] account for 3.5 percent of U.S. land area,[7] they also account for at least 60 percent of all IA/PA costs, including at least 80 percent of IA costs. As such, urban areas are places where mitigation projects can have a disproportionately large impact on costs. Table A.4 enumerates IA/PA expenditures for the ten most costly metro areas, broken down by disaster type. The data show that a relatively small number of metro areas account for a large portion of the total metro costs. The Houston and Miami metropolitan areas account for 20 percent of all costs attributable to a specific metro area, excluding costs from Katrina, Sandy, and Maria.[8] This is greater than the costs for the next seven metro areas combined. Moreover, these costs are not the result of a single incident. DRF expenditures in Houston and Miami (as well as New York City) have exceeded $100 million in four separate years during the 2004–2019 period.

The next three areas on the table—Beaumont (Texas), Baton Rouge (Louisiana), and Pensacola (Florida)—also account for a large portion of funds. Costs in each have exceeded $100 million in three separate years during the 2004–2019 period. Com-

6 For this analysis, we define urban areas as Census Bureau core-based statistical areas.

7 U.S. Census Bureau, "U.S. Cities Are Home to 62.7 Percent of the U.S. Population, but Comprise Just 3.5 Percent of Land Area," press release CB15-33, Washington, D.C., March 4, 2015.

8 Including those three, they would account for 10 percent and New Orleans/New York would account for 43 percent.

Table A.4
Public Assistance/Individual Assistance Expenditures for the Ten Most Costly Urban Areas, 2004–2019

Urban Area (MSA)	Percentage of Costs	Tropical Cyclone	Severe Storm	Flood	Snow	Fire	Ice Storm	Earthquake	Tornado
Houston, Tex.	11	4,929	63	143	0	1	0	0	0
Miami, Fla.	9	4,467	15	0	0	0	0	0	0
Beaumont, Tex.	4	1,743	1	5	0	0	0	0	0
Baton Rouge, La.	3	345	2	1,240	0	0	0	0	0
Pensacola, Fla.	3	1,446	137	0	0	0	0	0	0
Cedar Rapids, Iowa	3	0	1,365	9	0	0	2	0	0
Lake Charles, La.	2	1,117	3	6	0	0	0	0	0
New York, N.Y.	2	519	387	0	34	0	0	0	30
Orlando, Fla.	2	933	16	0	0	0	0	0	0
Chicago, Ill.	2	2	627	198	39	0	0	0	0

NOTE: Costs are in millions of 2019 dollars; excludes Hurricanes Katrina, Sandy, and Maria.

bined, they account for 10 percent of all costs attributable to a specific metro area, excluding costs from Katrina, Sandy, and Maria.

Texas, Florida, and Louisiana each have two metro areas on this top-ten list. This hints at the concentration of costs along the Gulf of Mexico. Imagine drawing a line along the coast from Galveston, Texas, to Miami, Florida. Excluding Katrina, Sandy, and Maria, 41 percent of the metro area costs were attributable to metro areas within 50 miles of that line.[9]

Summary

FEMA mitigation programs draw funds from DRF, and ideally save more than a dollar in DRF response costs for every dollar spent on program grants. This appendix examined DRF response costs from 1,974 disaster declarations over the 2004–2019 period using data sets from the OpenFEMA public data repository.

We find that extreme outlier disasters drive total DRF costs. Nineteen disaster declarations associated with Hurricanes Katrina, Sandy, and Maria account for more

[9] Including those three, 51 percent of costs were attributable to cities within 50 miles of that line.

costs than the other 1,955 declarations combined. We excluded these three events from the rest of the analyses because they are such extreme statistical outliers. Within the remaining declarations, we found that PA costs dominated spending, accounting for 72–86 percent of spending in each of the four-year periods between 2004 and 2019. Within PA, 39–58 percent of funding went toward temporary work (Categories A and B), and 29–49 percent went toward permanent work on roads, bridges, public buildings, and public utilities.[10] In terms of incident types, 58–96 percent of costs were attributable to tropical cyclones or severe storms. In terms of geography, 20 percent of costs attributable to a specific metro area were attributable to the Houston or Miami metropolitan areas, and 41 percent of costs were attributable to metro areas within 50 miles of the coastline stretching from Galveston to Miami.

Putting these factors together, the most significant cost drivers of DRF expenditures appear to be hurricanes and storms that damage roads, bridges, public buildings, and public utilities and/or are in low-elevation urban areas near the stretch of coast between Galveston and Miami. These account for 63 percent of all costs attributable to specific metro areas, excluding costs from Katrina, Sandy, and Maria.

---

[10] That is, FEMA PA project Categories C (roads and bridges), E (public buildings), and F (public utilities).

APPENDIX B

Indirect Benefits Technical Details

This appendix provides technical details supporting the findings and recommendations contained in Chapter Three. The appendix proceeds as follows. First, we walk through the canonical Leontief I-O model, which forms the basis of our near-term recommendation for estimating indirect benefits. We discuss the assumptions underlying the model, how it operates, how it can be used to examine the economic impacts of natural disaster and predisaster mitigation efforts, and look at the databases that support national and regional I-O analysis.

Next, we explore how to augment the traditional I-O model so that it is better suited for estimating the indirect economic benefits of BRIC projects. In particular, we describe how to supplement the baseline I-O model to capture sector resilience and "downstream" economic effects. To conclude our discussion of I-O models, we address how to compute key model inputs for BRIC projects. This naturally involves a discussion of how to leverage the existing capabilities in FEMA's Hazus program—a publicly available tool for natural hazard analysis.

Finally, we close the appendix with an overview of CGE models and their ability to estimate indirect benefits in the longer term. The overview contains an in-depth treatment of a canonical CGE model used for natural hazard analysis, a set of options for using CGE models to estimate indirect benefits, and a brief discussion of how to create an infrastructure to ease a possible transition from an I-O to CGE model for BRIC indirect benefits analysis.

The Leontief Input-Output Model

I-O models quantify the connectedness among sectors in a national or regional economy. More specifically, they capture the degree to which the goods and services (outputs) produced by each sector serve as inputs to the production processes of other sectors. The canonical model we present here is attributed to Wassily Leontief; since then, its formulation has been extended in a number of ways and used by policymakers in a wide variety of contexts.[1] A core feature of I-O models is their ability to trace how a change in the output of a given sector affects all the sectors providing production inputs to that sector and all the sectors providing inputs to those sectors and so on; ultimately, this allows one to estimate the effects of an initial industry-level change on the entire economy. This feature of I-O models makes them particularly attractive for quantifying the economic effects of natural disasters, especially because the models are supported by public data-collection efforts. To estimate the total economic effect of a natural disaster, one must account for its initial direct effect on various sectors, as well as how the initial disruption propagates throughout the broader economy. This methodology also provides a means of estimating the economic benefits of predisaster mitigation activities. Mitigation efforts dampen the initial disruption caused by a disaster, which then results in relatively lower indirect economic impacts compared to a counterfactual scenario where no mitigation measures took place. We turn to a detailed description of the model's underlying mechanics to convey how it produces these estimates.

Conceptual Framework

The following exposition draws on related content contained in Miller and Blair, 2009; the reader is referred to their work for further details. For this discussion, we assume that the economy we wish to study is a national economy—the U.S. economy, for example—over a given time frame, such as one year.[2] All economic activity in the United States (or any country, for that matter) over a given period can be partitioned among all the sectors (industries) that comprise it; there exist different (though related) sector classification schemes that define what these sectors are. Perhaps the two most prominent classification systems are the NAICS and the Standard Industrial Classification system, each of which provides a hierarchical categorization of economic sectors. That is, each contains an aggregated list of sectors that make up the economy—for example, mining and manufacturing—that may be expanded into more disaggregated lists, where sectors such as mining and manufacturing are broken down into increasingly more specific subcategories like coal mining and beverage manufacturing.

Within a given sector, the economic value of the output it produces can be divided into the value of its output that is used in production by other sectors—known as intermediate goods and services—and the value of its output that is consumed "as is" by end users, such as households, businesses, and the government. The latter category is referred to as final goods and services; it consists of items that are not used to produce

---

1 See, for example, Haimes et al., 2005a; Haimes et al., 2005b; Leontief, 1951a; Leontief, 1951b; Leontief, 1966; Lian and Haimes, 2006; Miller and Blair, 2009; and Okuyama and Santos, 2014.

2 We discuss how to apply these methods at the regional level and across different time horizons below.

other items. Hence, in an economy consisting of n sectors, we may express the value of the output of sector i, x_i, as

$$x_i = z_{i,1} + \cdots + z_{i,n} + f_i = \sum_{j=1}^{n} z_{i,j} + f_i, \tag{1}$$

where $z_{i,j}$ denotes the economic value of intermediate goods and services produced by sector i that are used in production by sector j and f_i denotes the total value of final demand of sector i output.[3] Since this categorization applies to all n sectors, we may write the corresponding equations for each sector to arrive at a system of equations describing the economic value of economywide production:

$$\begin{aligned} x_1 &= z_{1,1} + \cdots + z_{1,n} + f_1 \\ &\vdots \\ x_n &= z_{n,1} + \cdots + z_{n,n} + f_n. \end{aligned} \tag{2}$$

If we let

$$\boldsymbol{x} = \begin{bmatrix} x_1 \\ \vdots \\ x_n \end{bmatrix}, \boldsymbol{Z} = \begin{bmatrix} z_{1,1} & \cdots & z_{1,n} \\ \vdots & \ddots & \vdots \\ z_{n,1} & \cdots & z_{n,n} \end{bmatrix}, \boldsymbol{f} = \begin{bmatrix} f_1 \\ \vdots \\ f_n \end{bmatrix}, \textit{and } \boldsymbol{i} = \begin{bmatrix} 1 \\ \vdots \\ 1 \end{bmatrix}, \tag{3}$$

we may express more compactly the system of equations given in (2) as

$$\boldsymbol{x} = \boldsymbol{Z}\boldsymbol{i} + \boldsymbol{f}. \tag{4}$$

(Note that $\boldsymbol{i}$ is an $n \times 1$ column vector in which each row's value equals 1; this vector serves to sum each row in $\boldsymbol{Z}$.) We will follow the convention used above throughout the remainder of this appendix: bold lowercase letters will denote column vectors, and bold uppercase letters will signify matrices.

At this point, it is important to discuss two key assumptions underlying I-O models. First, production processes exhibit *constant returns to scale*, meaning that a doubling of production inputs will lead to a doubling of production outputs. Second, production inputs are not substitutable—particular inputs must be used in particular proportions to produce output. Note that the latter assumption implies that input proportions do not respond to changes in prices. To illustrate the first assumption, suppose that sector i is mining and sector j is manufacturing. Then, as described above, $z_{i,j}$

[3] Note that this allows for the possibility that sector i uses some of its own output as a production input.

represents the value of mining inputs purchased by the manufacturing sector for use in production and x_j represents the total value of manufacturing outputs over a given time frame. Next, define

$$a_{i,j} = \frac{z_{i,j}}{x_j}. \tag{5}$$

$a_{i,j}$ is referred to as the *technical coefficient* and denotes the dollar value of mining inputs needed to produce $1 worth of manufacturing output.[4] The constant returns to scale assumption is most easily seen by rearranging equation (5) such that $z_{i,j} = a_{i,j}x_j$. $a_{i,j}$ is assumed to be unchanging; thus, a doubling of outputs necessitates a doubling of inputs.[5]

We now demonstrate the second assumption. Suppose that the construction sector (sector k) uses inputs from both the mining and manufacturing sectors in production. $z_{i,k}$ thus denotes the value of inputs provided to the construction sector by the mining sector, and $z_{j,k}$ denotes the value of inputs provided to the construction sector by the manufacturing sector. The ratio of mining inputs to manufacturing inputs can be written as

$$\frac{z_{i,k}}{z_{j,k}} = \frac{a_{i,k}x_k}{a_{j,k}x_k} = \frac{a_{i,k}}{a_{j,k}}. \tag{6}$$

Because this equals a fixed number, we see that inputs must be used in fixed proportions in the I-O model. Now that we have addressed the critical assumptions that accompany the I-O approach, we will finish constructing the formulation of the model as it is used in practice, where the aim is often to project the impacts of industry-level changes in the production of final goods and services on the wider economy.

Using the definition of $a_{i,j}$ provided above, we can rewrite the system of equations given in (2) as

$$\begin{aligned} x_1 &= a_{1,1}x_1 + \cdots + a_{1,n}x_n + f_1 \\ &\vdots \\ x_n &= a_{n,1}x_1 + \cdots + a_{n,n}x_n + f_n. \end{aligned} \tag{7}$$

---

[4] To see this, suppose that $z_{i,j} = 100$ and $x_j = 1{,}000$. In this case, $a_{i,j} = 100/1{,}000 = 0.10/1$, meaning that $0.10 worth of mining inputs are needed to produce $1 worth of manufacturing output.

[5] Note that if $a_{i,j} = 0$ (i.e., the manufacturing sector does not use inputs from the mining sector in production), equation (5) implies that the value of x_j is infinite. To address this, the production function is typically specified as $x_j = \min\left\{\frac{z_{1,j}}{a_{1,j}}, \ldots, \frac{z_{n,j}}{a_{n,j}}\right\}$, which disallows infinite values of production output.

Next, collect all the technical coefficients in a technical coefficient matrix we will call $\boldsymbol{A}$:

$$\boldsymbol{A} = \begin{bmatrix} a_{1,1} & \cdots & a_{1,n} \\ \vdots & \ddots & \vdots \\ a_{n,1} & \cdots & a_{n,n} \end{bmatrix}. \tag{8}$$

With this definition of $\boldsymbol{A}$, the system of equations given in (7) can be succinctly written as

$$\boldsymbol{x} = \boldsymbol{A}\boldsymbol{x} + \boldsymbol{f}. \tag{9}$$

Our goal is to solve (9) for total production $\boldsymbol{x}$; we do so as follows. First, subtract the $\boldsymbol{Ax}$ term to the left side of the equation to obtain

$$\boldsymbol{x} - \boldsymbol{A}\boldsymbol{x} = \boldsymbol{f}. \tag{10}$$

Next, define the $n \times n$ identity matrix, $\boldsymbol{I}$, which is a matrix containing ones along the main diagonal and zeros elsewhere:

$$\boldsymbol{I} = \begin{bmatrix} 1 & \cdots & 0 \\ \vdots & \ddots & \vdots \\ 0 & \cdots & 1 \end{bmatrix}. \tag{11}$$

Any vector or matrix multiplied by $\boldsymbol{I}$ equals itself (provided the vector or matrix has the appropriate dimensions); thus, we may factor out the $\boldsymbol{x}$ term on the left side of the equation as such:

$$(\boldsymbol{I} - \boldsymbol{A})\boldsymbol{x} = \boldsymbol{f}. \tag{12}$$

Given a set of industry-level final goods and services figures $\boldsymbol{f}$, (12) represents a system of n equations containing n unknowns ($x_1, \ldots, x_n$). Provided that the inverse of $\boldsymbol{I} - \boldsymbol{A}$ exists, (12) has a unique solution. To solve this system of equations, premultiply both sides of (12) by $(\boldsymbol{I} - \boldsymbol{A})^{-1}$ to isolate the $\boldsymbol{x}$ term on the left side:

$$\boldsymbol{x} = (\boldsymbol{I} - \boldsymbol{A})^{-1}\boldsymbol{f} = \boldsymbol{L}\boldsymbol{f}. \tag{13}$$

(Recall that any matrix multiplied by its inverse equals the identity matrix.)

Equation (13) represents the canonical relationship in I-O models. ***L*** is known as the *Leontief inverse* or the *total requirements matrix*; its coefficients represent, for each industry, the value of total inputs required to produce one dollar of final goods and services. The equation illustrates how the model can be used to solve for the economic value of total industry output that is required to meet given levels of final output, ***f***: simply premultiply the final output vector by the total requirements matrix. We have now laid the groundwork necessary for the discussion in the next section, which covers how to calculate the effect that *changes* in final output in one or more sectors have on the broader economy. We specifically discuss how to use the I-O model to quantify the indirect economic benefits of predisaster mitigation activities.

Using the Input-Output Model to Quantify the Economic Benefits of Disaster Mitigation

Here, we cover how to use the I-O model described above to calculate the economic effects of a natural-disaster-induced disruption to one or more sectors of the economy, which then allows us to illustrate how to estimate the economic benefits of predisaster mitigation efforts. Disasters will cause a direct effect on final output for certain sectors, but to capture the true extent of the impact of a disaster on the economy, we must account for the inextricable linkages across economic sectors—indirect effects. As we have seen, this is a question well suited for I-O models. We discuss how to do so, both in a general, abstract sense and in the context of a simplified numerical example.

General Approach

We take as a starting point equation (13) above, because this is the equation most relevant for the task at hand. For the present discussion, it is useful to expand this expression into equation (14) below so that we may examine the individual elements of the vectors and matrix:

$$\begin{bmatrix} x_1 \\ \vdots \\ x_n \end{bmatrix} = \begin{bmatrix} L_{1,1} & \cdots & L_{1,n} \\ \vdots & \ddots & \vdots \\ L_{n,1} & \cdots & L_{n,n} \end{bmatrix} \begin{bmatrix} f_1 \\ \vdots \\ f_n \end{bmatrix}. \tag{14}$$

The specific conceptual question we are trying to answer is how a change in final output for a given sector (or set of sectors) affects total sectoral output for each sector in the economy, given the extent of intersectoral relationships observed in the data. For concreteness, suppose that sector i experiences a change in final output equal to Δf_i and final output for all other sectors remains unaffected. In a natural disaster, Δf_i will likely take a negative value, reflecting the fact that final output in sector i presumably decreases. The question then becomes figuring out how this change in sector i's final output affects total sectoral output x_j for all sectors j and, consequently, total economywide output.

Denote values after the disruption with a superscript "A" and values before the disruption with a superscript "B"; Δ designates the change in the value of a variable from before to after the disruption. Mathematically, answering this question amounts to the following:

$$\begin{bmatrix} x_1^A \\ \vdots \\ x_i^A \\ \vdots \\ x_n^A \end{bmatrix} - \begin{bmatrix} x_1^B \\ \vdots \\ x_i^B \\ \vdots \\ x_n^B \end{bmatrix} = \begin{bmatrix} \Delta x_1 \\ \vdots \\ \Delta x_i \\ \vdots \\ \Delta x_n \end{bmatrix} = \begin{bmatrix} L_{1,1} & \cdots & L_{1,n} \\ \vdots & \ddots & \vdots \\ L_{n,1} & \cdots & L_{n,n} \end{bmatrix} \begin{bmatrix} f_1^B \\ \vdots \\ f_i^B + \Delta f_i \\ \vdots \\ f_n^B \end{bmatrix} - \begin{bmatrix} L_{1,1} & \cdots & L_{1,n} \\ \vdots & \ddots & \vdots \\ L_{n,1} & \cdots & L_{n,n} \end{bmatrix} \begin{bmatrix} f_1^B \\ \vdots \\ f_i^B \\ \vdots \\ f_n^B \end{bmatrix} \tag{15}$$

$$= \begin{bmatrix} L_{1,1} & \cdots & L_{1,n} \\ \vdots & \ddots & \vdots \\ L_{n,1} & \cdots & L_{n,n} \end{bmatrix} \left(\begin{bmatrix} f_1^B \\ \vdots \\ f_i^B + \Delta f_i \\ \vdots \\ f_n^B \end{bmatrix} - \begin{bmatrix} f_1^B \\ \vdots \\ f_i^B \\ \vdots \\ f_n^B \end{bmatrix} \right)$$

$$= \begin{bmatrix} L_{1,1} & \cdots & L_{1,n} \\ \vdots & \ddots & \vdots \\ L_{n,1} & \cdots & L_{n,n} \end{bmatrix} \begin{bmatrix} 0 \\ \vdots \\ \Delta f_i \\ \vdots \\ 0 \end{bmatrix}.$$

By defining the following vectors,

$$\Delta \boldsymbol{x} \begin{bmatrix} \Delta x_1 \\ \vdots \\ \Delta x_i \\ \vdots \\ \Delta x_n \end{bmatrix} = \text{and } \Delta \mathbf{f} = \begin{bmatrix} 0 \\ \vdots \\ \Delta f_i \\ \vdots \\ 0 \end{bmatrix}, \tag{16}$$

the final expression in (15) can be written as

$$\Delta \boldsymbol{x} = \boldsymbol{L}\Delta \boldsymbol{f}. \tag{17}$$

The above derivation is interpreted as follows. Recall that we are interested in determining the *change* in total sectoral output resulting from an initial change in sector *i*'s final output. This naturally lends itself to a "before-and-after" comparison: If we know total sectoral output after the disruption, we can subtract the level of total sectoral output before the disruption to determine how the disruption changes total output throughout the economy. The change in total sectoral output is represented by the left side of the first equation in (15); the notation Δx_j represents the difference in x_j before and after the disruption. From (14), we know how a given total sectoral output vector relates to the total requirements matrix and final output vector—it is the product of the two. Therefore, the change in total sectoral output equals the product of the total requirements matrix and the final output vector after the disruption minus the product of the total requirements matrix and the final output vector before the disruption.

Note that the final output vector after the disruption is largely the same as the final output vector before the disruption; the only difference is the change to sector *i*'s final output, which we have denoted by Δf_i. Because the total requirements matrix is constant across the before-and-after scenarios, we may factor out this term, as shown in the second line of (15). Finally, because the only difference between the final output vectors lies in the addition of Δf_i to sector *i*'s final output (reflecting the disruption to this sector), subtracting the final output vector before the disruption from the corresponding vector after the disruption results in a column vector of zeros (save for the value of Δf_i), which populates the *i*th row of the vector. The same steps would be used to estimate the effects of initial disruptions to multiple industries. In this case, the final output vector after the disruption would have a Δf_j term added to the final output of each industry *j* that experiences a disruption, where the value of this term will vary across industries, depending on the extent to which each industry is disrupted.

We have now illustrated precisely how to use the I-O model to quantify the economic effects of a natural disaster: postmultiply the total requirements matrix by a vector containing the change in final output of the affected sectors. The total requirements matrix hence serves to calibrate the expected effect of a change in the final output of a given sector on each sector that supplies it, either directly or indirectly, with production inputs. The aggregate economic effect can be estimated by summing the individual elements within $\Delta \boldsymbol{x}$, because each element is denominated in the same monetary unit. Indirect effects, however, can be isolated by subtracting the direct effects vector, $\Delta \boldsymbol{f}$, from the total effects vector, $\Delta \boldsymbol{x}$. Note that, in the end, we did not need information on final output by sector before the disruption; we only needed information on the change in final sectoral output before and after the disruption.

The multipliers embedded in the total requirements matrix described above are often referred to as Type I multipliers, which reflect only the indirect economic effects on industries. By incorporating data on payments to labor and capital, one can move from a "closed" I-O model—the model we have been describing—to an "open" I-O model. Open I-O models can additionally estimate "induced effects" by capturing projected effects on income, which subsequently impact demand for final goods and services. Type II multipliers encapsulate both industry and induced effects. The use of data on payments to labor and capital also allows Type I multipliers to be calculated in terms of value added instead of output, where value added is roughly equivalent to gross regional product. Output-based I-O multipliers will double count some economic effects because the value of intermediate goods and services is also reflected in the prices of the final goods and services they were used to produce. Value-added multipliers avoid double counting by only estimating the effects on value added at each stage of the production process. The BEA publishes publicly available data on payments to labor and capital. These data are also contained in SAMs. Value-added Type I multipliers and Type II multipliers can be derived using largely the same steps we have described, provided data on payments to labor and capital are contained in the underlying I-O table.

It is important to emphasize that the indirect effects captured by the traditional I-O model only include "upstream" or "backward" supply chain effects—the effects of a change in sector *i*'s final output on its direct and indirect suppliers—and not "downstream" or "forward" supply chain effects on the sectors it is a supplier for. To see this, note that equation (15) reduces to the following:

$$\begin{bmatrix} \Delta x_1 \\ \vdots \\ \Delta x_n \end{bmatrix} = \begin{bmatrix} L_{1,i}\Delta f_i \\ \vdots \\ L_{n,i}\Delta f_i \end{bmatrix}. \tag{18}$$

The elements of the total requirements matrix—and the technical coefficients matrix from which it was derived—capture the inputs *to* a given sector that are required for it to produce output. Hence, in equation (18), any element $L_{j,i}\Delta f_i$ on the right side of the expression will capture the effect of a change in the final output of sector *i* on the inputs provided to sector *i* by sector *j*. A more complete estimate of total economic effects would account for downstream effects as well; we explore one method for doing so during our discussion of model extensions contained later in this appendix.

There remains the question of how to use the I-O model to quantify the economic benefits of predisaster mitigation efforts. This is accomplished by using the same type of estimation strategy sketched above. Conceptually, the projected economic benefits of predisaster mitigation activities are the expected difference between the value of lost economic output resulting from a natural disaster scenario when no such activities took place beforehand and the value of lost economic output resulting from the same disaster scenario when these activities had taken place beforehand. The difference between these two numbers represents the projected total economic value of the mitigation efforts—the value of sectoral output that would have been lost if the mitigation efforts had not been undertaken.

Let variables containing a superscript "N" denote variables corresponding to the scenario when mitigation activities did not take place and let variables containing a superscript "Y" denote variables corresponding to the scenario when mitigation activities did take place. Consequently, Δf_i^N denotes the expected change in the value of final output experienced by sector i if no mitigation took place and Δf_i^Y denotes the change in the value of final output experienced by sector i if mitigation did take place. Assume that $|\Delta f_i^N| > |\Delta f_i^Y|$, meaning that sector i experiences a greater disruption in the absence of efforts to mitigate the effects of a disaster before it occurs. The change in the value of total output induced by a disaster without prior mitigation efforts is given by

$$\begin{bmatrix} x_1^{A,N} \\ \vdots \\ x_i^{A,N} \\ \vdots \\ x_n^{A,N} \end{bmatrix} - \begin{bmatrix} x_1^{B} \\ \vdots \\ x_i^{B} \\ \vdots \\ x_n^{B} \end{bmatrix} = \begin{bmatrix} \Delta x_1^{N} \\ \vdots \\ \Delta x_i^{N} \\ \vdots \\ \Delta x_n^{N} \end{bmatrix} = \begin{bmatrix} L_{1,1} \cdots L_{1,n} \\ \vdots \ \ddots \ \vdots \\ L_{n,1} \cdots L_{n,n} \end{bmatrix} \begin{bmatrix} f_1^{B} \\ \vdots \\ f_i^{B} + \Delta f_i^N \\ \vdots \\ f_n^{B} \end{bmatrix} - \begin{bmatrix} L_{1,1} \cdots L_{1,n} \\ \vdots \ \ddots \ \vdots \\ L_{n,1} \cdots L_{n,n} \end{bmatrix} \begin{bmatrix} f_1^{B} \\ \vdots \\ f_i^{B} \\ \vdots \\ f_n^{B} \end{bmatrix} \tag{19}$$

$$= \begin{bmatrix} L_{1,1} \cdots L_{1,n} \\ \vdots \ \ddots \ \vdots \\ L_{n,1} \cdots L_{n,n} \end{bmatrix} \left(\begin{bmatrix} f_1^{B} \\ \vdots \\ f_i^{B} + \Delta f_i^N \\ \vdots \\ f_n^{B} \end{bmatrix} - \begin{bmatrix} f_1^{B} \\ \vdots \\ f_i^{B} \\ \vdots \\ f_n^{B} \end{bmatrix} \right)$$

$$= \begin{bmatrix} L_{1,1} \cdots L_{1,n} \\ \vdots \ \ddots \ \vdots \\ L_{n,1} \cdots L_{n,n} \end{bmatrix} \begin{bmatrix} 0 \\ \vdots \\ \Delta f_i^N \\ \vdots \\ 0 \end{bmatrix}.$$

The change in the value of total output induced by a disaster with prior mitigation efforts follows a similar derivation, ultimately resulting in

$$\begin{bmatrix} x_1^{A,Y} \\ \vdots \\ x_i^{A,Y} \\ \vdots \\ x_n^{A,Y} \end{bmatrix} - \begin{bmatrix} x_1^{B} \\ \vdots \\ x_i^{B} \\ \vdots \\ x_n^{B} \end{bmatrix} = \begin{bmatrix} \Delta x_1^{Y} \\ \vdots \\ \Delta x_i^{Y} \\ \vdots \\ \Delta x_n^{Y} \end{bmatrix} = \begin{bmatrix} L_{1,1} \cdots L_{1,n} \\ \vdots \ \ddots \ \vdots \\ L_{n,1} \cdots L_{n,n} \end{bmatrix} \begin{bmatrix} 0 \\ \vdots \\ \Delta f_i^{Y} \\ \vdots \\ 0 \end{bmatrix}. \tag{20}$$

We can then use the expressions derived above to estimate the total economic benefits of the disaster mitigation efforts as follows:

$$\begin{aligned} \begin{bmatrix} \Delta x_1^{N} \\ \vdots \\ \Delta x_i^{N} \\ \vdots \\ \Delta x_n^{N} \end{bmatrix} - \begin{bmatrix} \Delta x_1^{Y} \\ \vdots \\ \Delta x_i^{Y} \\ \vdots \\ \Delta x_n^{Y} \end{bmatrix} &= \begin{bmatrix} L_{1,1} \cdots L_{1,n} \\ \vdots \ \ddots \ \vdots \\ L_{n,1} \cdots L_{n,n} \end{bmatrix} \begin{bmatrix} 0 \\ \vdots \\ \Delta f_i^{N} \\ \vdots \\ 0 \end{bmatrix} - \begin{bmatrix} L_{1,1} \cdots L_{1,n} \\ \vdots \ \ddots \ \vdots \\ L_{n,1} \cdots L_{n,n} \end{bmatrix} \begin{bmatrix} 0 \\ \vdots \\ \Delta f_i^{Y} \\ \vdots \\ 0 \end{bmatrix} \\ &= \begin{bmatrix} L_{1,1} \cdots L_{1,n} \\ \vdots \ \ddots \ \vdots \\ L_{n,1} \cdots L_{n,n} \end{bmatrix} \left(\begin{bmatrix} 0 \\ \vdots \\ \Delta f_i^{N} \\ \vdots \\ 0 \end{bmatrix} - \begin{bmatrix} 0 \\ \vdots \\ \Delta f_i^{Y} \\ \vdots \\ 0 \end{bmatrix} \right) \\ &= \begin{bmatrix} L_{1,1} \cdots L_{1,n} \\ \vdots \ \ddots \ \vdots \\ L_{n,1} \cdots L_{n,n} \end{bmatrix} \left(\begin{bmatrix} 0 \\ \vdots \\ \Delta f_i^{N} - \Delta f_i^{Y} \\ \vdots \\ 0 \end{bmatrix} \right). \end{aligned} \tag{21}$$

Note that the only information required to undertake this calculation is the total requirements matrix and the difference between the direct industry impact with and without prior mitigation efforts.

The I-O modeling approach can be easily adapted to analyze different time horizons. In the general examples discussed above, the unit of observation was a given country (the United States) over a given time frame (one year). Implicitly, our industry disruption Δf_i was a disruption to annual final industry output and the resulting economic effects we calculated were scaled at the annual level as well. But what if a disruption lasted more or less than one year? What if we wanted to allow for a sector to gradually recover over a given time frame? One approach to tackling these questions is to discretize the model into finer or coarser segments depending on the analytical goal.

For example, suppose we wanted to analyze the effects of a disruption to an industry that lasts for six months; suppose further that, initially, the final output decreases by \$60 million and recovers by \$10 million with each passing month. To estimate the total economic effects of this disruption, we could (1) divide our annual sectoral data by 12 to translate the data to a monthly level; (2) estimate six separate monthly I-O models, where the sectoral disruption in each model ranges from –\$60 million in the first month to –\$10 million in the sixth and final month before recovery; and (3) sum the total economic effects across each model. In this example, we assumed that annual sectoral output was roughly evenly distributed across months when moving from an annual to monthly unit of observation; in practice, sectoral production may exhibit seasonal patterns. More generally, the data can be scaled in any number of ways and recovery paths can be specified as the analyst sees fit—be they parametric functions or manually entered values. When analyzing disruptions lasting longer than one year, estimates of economic effects should be reported as the present discounted value to account for the time value of money. In the next section, we present a simplified numerical example to demonstrate how to apply I-O methods in practice.

Numerical Example

What follows is a detailed walk-through of how to use the I-O model described above to estimate the economic benefits of predisaster mitigation activities in a hypothetical two-sector economy. Consider an economy consisting of only two sectors: utilities (sector one) and retail trade (sector two). We have the following annual, U.S. dollar-denominated industry-level data for this economy:

$$\boldsymbol{Z} = \begin{bmatrix} 800 & 300 \\ 200 & 240 \end{bmatrix}, \boldsymbol{f} = \begin{bmatrix} 900 \\ 760 \end{bmatrix}, \text{ and } \boldsymbol{x} = \begin{bmatrix} 2000 \\ 1200 \end{bmatrix}. \tag{22}$$

Recall that these variables are interpreted as follows. Any element $z_{i,j}$ in the matrix $\boldsymbol{Z}$ represents the value of the intermediate goods and services produced by sector i that are used in production by sector j. Take, for example, $z_{1,2}$, which equals 300. This tells us that the retail trade industry uses \$300 worth of inputs from the utilities sector to produce its annual output. Each row in $\boldsymbol{f}$ denotes the value of final goods and services produced by a sector. Hence, in our example, the utilities sector produces \$900 worth of final goods and services, and the retail trade sector produces \$760 worth of final goods and services. $\boldsymbol{x}$ captures the total value of industry production—that is, the sum of the values of intermediate and final goods and services production. Each row of $\boldsymbol{x}$ therefore equals the sum of the corresponding rows in $\boldsymbol{Z}$ and $\boldsymbol{f}$. Ultimately, as illustrated in the preceding section, we want to drive toward a model of the form

$$\boldsymbol{x} = (\boldsymbol{I} - \boldsymbol{A})^{-1} \boldsymbol{f} = \boldsymbol{L}\boldsymbol{f}. \tag{13}$$

$$\Delta \boldsymbol{x} = (\boldsymbol{I} - \boldsymbol{A})^{-1} \Delta \boldsymbol{f} = \boldsymbol{L} \Delta \boldsymbol{f}. \tag{17}$$

Thus, we now proceed to construct the $\boldsymbol{L}$ (total requirements) matrix. Following this, we lay out the parameters governing our hypothetical disaster scenario.

Given that $\boldsymbol{L}$ is a function of $\boldsymbol{A}$—the technical coefficients matrix—we first need to calculate the elements of $\boldsymbol{A}$. Earlier, we noted that each element $a_{i,j}$ of $\boldsymbol{A}$ denotes the dollar value of inputs from industry i needed to make \$1 worth of sector j output; $a_{i,j}$ is calculated by taking the ratio of $z_{i,j}$ to x_j. This means we can calculate the individual elements of $\boldsymbol{A}$ by dividing each element in $\boldsymbol{Z}$ by the value of total output of its corresponding "column" industry. This results in

$$\boldsymbol{A} = \begin{bmatrix} \frac{800}{2000} = 0.4 & \frac{300}{1200} = 0.25 \\ \frac{200}{2000} = 0.1 & \frac{240}{1200} = 0.2 \end{bmatrix}, \tag{23}$$

which implies that

$$\boldsymbol{I} - \boldsymbol{A} = \begin{bmatrix} 1 & 0 \\ 0 & 1 \end{bmatrix} - \begin{bmatrix} 0.4 & 0.25 \\ 0.1 & 0.2 \end{bmatrix} = \begin{bmatrix} 0.6 & -0.25 \\ -0.1 & 0.8 \end{bmatrix}. \tag{24}$$

Taking the inverse of this matrix, we obtain the total requirements matrix (values are rounded to two decimal places):

$$(\boldsymbol{I} - \boldsymbol{A})^{-1} = \boldsymbol{L} = \begin{bmatrix} 1.76 & 0.55 \\ 0.22 & 1.32 \end{bmatrix}. \tag{25}$$

We have now constructed the I-O model that we use to estimate the benefits of a particular disaster mitigation scenario:

$$\begin{bmatrix} 2000 \\ 1200 \end{bmatrix} = \begin{bmatrix} 1.76 & 0.55 \\ 0.22 & 1.32 \end{bmatrix} \begin{bmatrix} 900 \\ 760 \end{bmatrix}. \tag{26}$$

The scenario we will examine is described as follows. Suppose that if a particular disaster were to occur—and no predisaster mitigation activities took place beforehand—monthly final utilities output would initially decrease by two-thirds and remain at that level for six months. Then, final output would partially recover such that monthly production would be one-third less than normal. Final output would remain at this new level for six months before the utilities sector fully recovered to its predisaster final output rate. If, however, this same disaster were to occur and mitigation activities had taken place beforehand, final output would initially drop by only one-half and remain at that level for six months. It would then recover to a level one-fourth less than normal for the following six months before fully recovering. We assume that annual production is evenly distributed across months, meaning that annual utilities final output of \$900 equates to monthly production of \$75.[6] The utilities sector recovery paths with and without predisaster mitigation are depicted in Figure B.1.

Our goal is to estimate the economic value of the predisaster mitigation efforts in the context of this disaster scenario. We break down the economic value of these efforts into (1) direct economic benefits, (2) indirect economic benefits, and (3) total economic benefits. To compute each, we will follow the approach described in the preceding sec-

Figure B.1
Utilities Sector Recovery Paths

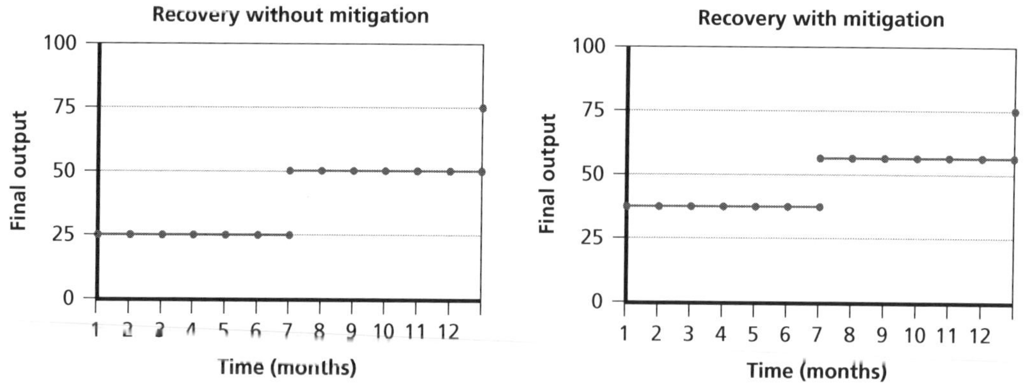

---

[6] In reality, annual production may not be evenly distributed across months. For example, production in a given industry may exhibit seasonal patterns.

tion. First, we estimate projected direct, indirect, and total economic losses resulting from the disaster in the absence of predisaster mitigation. We do so by estimating two I-O models—one that captures the disruption experienced during the first six months and one that captures the disruption experienced during the last six months. In the former case, the initial disruption to (or direct effect on) the utilities sector equals –50. This is constructed by subtracting 75 (the predisaster value of monthly final output) from 25 (the value of monthly final output during the six months following the disaster). Since this disruption lasts for six months, the direct effects on the utilities sector of the disaster equal –50 multiplied by 6, or –\$300. The direct economic effects on the retail trade sector equal zero, because this sector is not directly affected by the disaster. To calculate the total economic effects during this time frame, we estimate the I-O model below via matrix multiplication:

$$\begin{bmatrix} \Delta x_1^{N,1} \\ \Delta x_2^{N,1} \end{bmatrix} = \left(\begin{bmatrix} 1.76 & 0.55 \\ 0.22 & 1.32 \end{bmatrix} \begin{bmatrix} -50 \\ 0 \end{bmatrix} \right) \times 6 = \begin{bmatrix} -528 \\ -66 \end{bmatrix}. \tag{27}$$

The superscript "N" denotes variables corresponding to the scenario in which no predisaster mitigation occurred; the superscript "1" denotes variables associated with the first six months following the disaster. As was the case when estimating the direct effects, total effects are multiplied by six, because the same sectoral disruption occurs for six consecutive months. The projected total economic effect on the utilities sector during the first six months after the disaster is therefore –\$528, while the projected total economic effect on the retail trade sector is –\$66. To calculate the indirect economic effect of the disaster on each sector, we subtract, for each sector, the direct effect from the total effect. Hence, during the six months immediately following the disaster, the indirect economic effect on the utilities sector equals –\$228, and the indirect economic effect on the retail trade sector equals –\$66. Note that for the retail trade sector, the total and indirect economic effects are one and the same given that this sector does not experience a direct disruption.

We follow the same procedure to estimate direct, indirect, and total economic losses by sector during the last six months of the disruption. The only difference is that the disruption that now enters into the model for the utilities sector equals 50 – 75, or –25. Hence, the direct economic loss to the utilities sector equals –\$150 during the latter six months, while the direct economic loss to the retail trade sector remains at zero. Total economic effects by sector are calculated as follows:

$$\begin{bmatrix} \Delta x_1^{N,2} \\ \Delta x_2^{N,2} \end{bmatrix} = \left(\begin{bmatrix} 1.76 & 0.55 \\ 0.22 & 1.32 \end{bmatrix} \begin{bmatrix} -25 \\ 0 \end{bmatrix} \right) \times 6 \qquad (28)$$

$$= \begin{bmatrix} -264 \\ -33 \end{bmatrix}.$$

This implies that the total economic effect on the utilities sector during the latter six months equals –$264, meaning the indirect economic effect on this sector during this window equals –$114. As before, total and indirect economic effects on the retail trade sector are the same and equal –$33 during the final six months of the disruption.

The economic effects of the disaster on each sector in the absence of predisaster mitigation efforts equal the sum of the effects during the first and last six-month periods. The utilities sector is projected to experience direct, indirect, and total economic losses of $450, $342, and $792, respectively. The retail trade sector is projected to experience no direct economic losses and indirect economic losses equal to –$99, resulting in a total economic loss of –$99 in the absence of predisaster mitigation. The remainder of our task is to compute these same figures for the scenario in which predisaster mitigation activities did take place and compare them to the numbers we computed above.

According to the scenario description given earlier, when predisaster mitigation measures take place prior to the disaster, the utilities sector is projected to experience a –$37.50 drop in monthly final output during each of the first six months following the disaster (i.e., a 50-percent reduction relative to its predisaster value). During the next six months, the utilities sector is projected to recover such that monthly final output is only –$18.75 (i.e., 25 percent) below its predisaster value. We may therefore estimate direct, indirect, and total economic losses to each sector in the presence of predisaster mitigation measures using the same approach as before. The difference is that, in this case, the direct disruption to monthly final utilities sector output equals –$37.50 during the first six months following the disaster and –$18.75 during the last six months of the recovery. The resulting estimates are as follows. The utilities sector is projected to experience direct, indirect, and total economic losses equal to $337.50, $256.50, and $594, respectively. The retail trade sector, however, is not expected to have any direct losses, although it is expected to endure indirect and, therefore, total economic losses amounting to $74.25.

Tables B.1 and B.2 summarize the results of our analysis by sector; Table B.3 sums the economic losses results across sectors to provide estimates at the economy-wide level. The main findings for our hypothetical disaster scenario are reported in the last two rows of Table B.3 and are the following: The I-O model projects that mitigation activities will reduce direct economic losses by $112.50, indirect economic losses by $110.25, and total economic losses by $222.75 compared to the counterfactual scenario in which the same disaster event occurred but no mitigation efforts had taken place beforehand. This amounts to a 25-percent reduction in lost economic value.

Through this example, we have demonstrated how the I-O model can be used in practice to estimate the direct, indirect, and total economic effects of disasters and predisaster mitigation activities. The approach we have described in the context of this simplified two-sector economy generalizes to the case in which we consider all sectors of an economy. First, data on $\boldsymbol{Z}$ and $\boldsymbol{x}$ would be used to create the $\boldsymbol{A}$ and $\boldsymbol{L}$ matrices, using the same steps as above. The only difference would be that $\boldsymbol{Z}$ and $\boldsymbol{x}$ would be of greater dimensions in the all-sector case, reflecting the greater number of sectors being considered relative to our example. Accordingly, the $\boldsymbol{A}$ and $\boldsymbol{L}$ matrices would also be of greater dimensions relative to the two-by-two matrices in the example. Calculating the economic effects of a disaster and predisaster mitigation efforts would proceed as above; again, the only difference would lie in the dimensions of the vectors and matrices making up the model. Total, direct, and indirect economic effects would be computed by summing the respective sector-level effects across sectors, as in the example.

Importantly, the model is relatively straightforward to implement and can be designed to keep required user expertise at a minimum; much of what we have described can be automated. The I-O model thus represents a potentially powerful tool to support BRIC program decisionmaking by providing a feasible means to capture the economic benefits to the broader community of predisaster mitigation efforts. Next, we examine the national and regional databases that support I-O analysis. We then conclude our discussion of I-O methods by considering practical means to refine the traditional model.

Supporting Databases

This section focuses on detailing the data that the I-O model requires. We begin with a discussion of national, publicly available databases. We cover where the data are located, the variables the data contain, the structure the data take, and how the data can be used in I-O analysis. Following this discussion, we focus the data available to estimate I-O models at the regional level. What follows draws on information contained in Haimes et al., 2005a.[7]

National Input-Output Data

Recall that, ultimately, the I-O model simply requires the total requirements matrix and projected changes in final output by sector. BEA publishes the national total requirements matrix at a number of different NAICS industry aggregation levels; this

[7] Haimes et al., 2005a.

Table B.1
Utilities Sector Economic Losses Following a Disaster

Scenario	Direct Losses	Indirect Losses	Total Losses
Without mitigation	$450	$342	$792
With mitigation	$337.50	$256.50	$594
Level difference	$112.50	$85.50	$198
Percentage difference	25%	25%	25%

Table B.2
Retail Trade Sector Economic Losses Following a Disaster

Scenario	Direct Losses	Indirect Losses	Total Losses
Without mitigation	$0	$99	$99
With mitigation	$0	$74.25	$74.25
Level difference	$0	$24.75	$24.75
Percentage difference	N/A	25%	25%

Table B.3
Economywide Economic Losses Following a Disaster

Scenario	Direct Losses	Indirect Losses	Total Losses
Without mitigation	$450	$441	$891
With mitigation	$337.50	$330.75	$668.25
Level difference	$112.50	$110.25	$222.75
Percentage difference	25%	25%	25%

substantially streamlines the process of estimating national-level I-O models.[8] One can also create the total requirements matrix using the methods described earlier in this appendix by leveraging the underlying data on interindustry economic flows, which BEA also publishes at the national level. Understanding how to use the interindustry flows data can be useful, particularly when considering variants of the traditional I-O model, such as the means for projecting downstream economic impacts described below. That model does not make use of the total requirements matrix, but it does use a related matrix constructed from the same underlying industry-level data. For con-

[8] Specifically, BEA has estimated the total requirements matrix for the 15-, 71-, and 405-industry economies. The different levels of aggregation reflect the hierarchical categorization of industries; that is, the 15-industry economy is expanded into increasingly more specific industry subcategories in order to produce the matrices for the 71- and 405-industry economies.

creteness, we now describe the underlying industry-level data against the backdrop of the total requirements matrix.

The total requirements matrix is a function of the technical coefficients matrix. As defined above, each element $a_{i,j}$ of the technical coefficients matrix represents the dollar value of inputs from industry i needed by industry j to produce one dollar of output. The rows of the matrix thus represent, for each industry, the value of intermediate output from that industry required to make one dollar of output in every industry. Hence, each row can be thought of as representing the contribution of a given industry to the "production recipes" of each industry. The columns of the matrix represent, for each industry, the value of inputs needed by that industry from each industry to make one dollar of output—that is, columns depict, for each industry, its "consumption" of inputs from every industry.

BEA provides information on the value of goods and services produced and consumed by each sector of the U.S. economy, but constructing the technical coefficients matrix is not quite as simple as what was described above, where we constructed $a_{i,j}$ by dividing $z_{i,j}$ by x_j. In our earlier discussion, we implicitly assumed that each industry produces one unique commodity, which simplified the task of calculating the technical coefficients. In reality, a given industry may produce more than one commodity, and a given commodity may be produced by more than one industry. BEA captures this information in Make-Use tables. The Make matrix reports the value of the different commodities produced by each industry, while the Use matrix reports the value of the different commodities consumed by each industry. The Make-Use tables can be manipulated to construct the technical coefficients matrix and, consequently, the total requirements matrix. See Haimes et al., 2005a, for further details.[9] Related models such as the downstream effects model detailed in the following section also use data on $z_{i,j}$ and x_j; the data necessary to estimate these models can therefore be extracted from the Make-Use tables as well.

Regional Input-Output Data

In a broad sense, regional I-O analysis is conducted by "regionalizing" the national-level technical coefficient matrix. This is accomplished by using *location quotients*, which compare an industry's concentration within a region to the industry's concentration nationwide. More specifically, a location quotient is calculated by taking the ratio of an industry's share of a regional economic statistic to the industry's share of the corresponding national figure. For most industries, wages and salaries are used to compute location quotients. The location quotients are then used to scale the national technical coefficient matrix to the regional level according to how the industrial concentration within a region differs from its national counterpart. Once the regional technical coefficient matrix has been constructed, standard I-O methods can be applied. See

[9] Haimes et al., 2005a.

Haimes et al., 2005a, for more information on how to use location quotients to create regional technical coefficient matrices.[10] The U.S. Bureau of Labor Statistics publishes location quotients down to the county level, which may be downloaded from its webpage.[11] Location quotients can also be used to "regionalize" related models—such as the downstream effects model described below—using a similar approach.

BEA's RIMS II provides another means to estimate regional economic effects. RIMS II is an I-O framework that also leverages the concept of location quotients to produce economic impact estimates at the regional level. What distinguishes RIMS II is that the model has already been developed and used to produce regional estimates that are succinctly summarized by a set of *multipliers*. The multipliers immediately allow the user to determine how a change in the final output of one or more industries affects total gross output, value added, earnings, and employment at the regional level. A region is defined as an area consisting of one or more contiguous counties. The ease of use provided by RIMS II comes with a price; when writing this report, RIMS II multipliers cost $275 per region or $75 per industry. Purchasing RIMS II multipliers for a region yields multipliers for all industries within the region, while purchasing multipliers for an industry provides multipliers for that industry for each of the 50 states, plus the District of Columbia. For more information on the BEA RIMS II model, see the RIMS II user guide.[12] Note that like the Leontief I-O model, the RIMS II model only captures indirect economic effects resulting from "upstream" or "backward" supply chain impacts.

Disaggregating to the regional level is important to capture the unique characteristics of the regional economy hit by the disaster to avoid estimation errors. Aggregation errors will always be present given the finite limit of the number of industrial accounts in the matrix; however, the more disaggregated the I-O table, the higher the ability to reduce aggregation errors.[13] Disaggregation of the sectors does present issues in itself where the complex interconnectedness of the region with its surrounding neighbors can be challenging to capture.[14] For instance, the ability for I-O tables to capture interregional and international trade is limited. Economic trade is an important component of any regional economy, and failure to capture trade can lead to estimation errors.[15] Additionally, using regional-level data presents temporal limitations where data are either out of date from time-intensive collection periods or because the

---

[10] Haimes et al., 2005a.

[11] U.S. Bureau of Labor Statistics, 2020.

[12] Bureau of Economic Analysis, *RIMS II: An Essential Tool for Regional Developers and Planners*, Washington, D.C.: U.S. Department of Commerce, 2013.

[13] Albala-Bertrand, 2014.

[14] Albala-Bertrand, 2014.

[15] Coughlin and Mandelbaum, 1991; Albala-Bertrand, 2014.

BEA data are only updated every five years or so. If the economic structure of the study region changes in the time between data collection and analysis, there could be estimation errors. Economies often change because of technology, new inventions or methods of production, industrial expansion, or price changes. As a result, such temporal factors can limit the accuracy of I-O analyses.[16]

Additionally, there are computational constraints on how the errors interact during the calculations that take place when the model is solved where the errors can create bias in the estimates.[17] It is therefore important for the analyst to be aware of these constraints when modeling regional economic impacts of natural disasters to estimate the indirect benefits. Maintaining awareness of the uncertainties—coupled with the analyst's expertise on the region, the data, and the model—can help minimize estimation errors and manage uncertainty in the results given these constraints.

Refining the Input-Output Model for Building Resilient Infrastructure and Community Indirect Benefits Analysis

Now that we have described the structure and mechanics of the traditional I-O model—as well as the databases that support it—we present recommended technical modifications to the baseline model. First, we recommend augmenting the model to incorporate *economic resilience* at the industry (sector) level. The baseline I-O model detailed above is a static (as opposed to dynamic) model, meaning it does account for time-varying changes in the economic environment. Hence, the core model does not capture economic resilience, defined by Rose, Oladosu, and Liao, 2007, as the ability of firms, industries, or regional economies to moderate the realized impacts of a disruption through inherent and adaptive responses.[18] This is an important dimension to capture in the disaster and predisaster mitigation context; if our goal is to project as accurately as possible the economic effects of disasters and disaster mitigation efforts, we must consider the ability of industries to respond to disruptions.

Second, we recommend altering the model's design to capture "downstream" or "forward" supply chain effects. This results in a related model that would be estimated in addition to the Leontief I-O model; both would be supplemented to account for sector resilience. As noted above, the traditional I-O model only accounts for indirect economic effects arising from impacts on upstream suppliers because of its inherent structure. Adding downstream effects into the equation provides another means to enhance the fidelity of the economic impact estimates. We also address the two key model inputs: the initial sectoral disruption and the presumed sector recovery paths.

---

16 Bess and Ambargis, 2011; Albala-Bertrand, 2014.

17 Bullard and Sebald, 1988; Lenzen, Wood, and Wiedmann, 2010.

18 Rose, Oladosu, and Liao, 2007.

In all of our previous discussion, we have assumed that the analyst has been given these numbers and functions. In practice, however, the analyst must determine these to ready the model for analysis.

Incorporating Sector Resilience

Our proposed method for incorporating sector resilience into the I-O model leverages existing approaches for estimating to what degree sectors are able to lessen the impacts of various disruptions. We illustrate the proposed method in the context of the estimates produced by Rose, Oladosu, and Liao, 2007.[19] Rose, Oladosu, and Shu-Yi Liao aim to estimate the business interruption losses that would result from a total electricity blackout in Los Angeles, California, lasting two weeks. They pay particular attention to the roles that economic resilience (defined above) and indirect effects (ripple effects beyond the firms who directly lose electricity) play in the resulting estimates. The authors construct their business interruption losses estimates using a Los Angeles–specific CGE model.

During their analysis, the authors estimate *sector resilience* coefficients that can be mapped to the two-digit NAICS level. They measure direct resilience by calculating the "deviation from the proportional relationship between the percentage utility disruption and the percentage reduction in customer output for a given period."[20] That is to say, in the absence of any sectoral resilience, an *x*-percent decrease in electricity service would lead to a direct economic loss of *x*-percent for a given sector. Resilience is calculated as the difference between this relationship and the relationship estimated in their model. Overall sector resilience is a function of a number of underlying variables, which can be organized into two categories: inherent resilience and adaptive resilience. Inherent resilience represents the ability to attenuate the impacts of a disruption under normal circumstances, while adaptive resilience captures the ability to lessen the impacts in crisis scenarios when there is increased impetus to put in extra effort or find creative solutions to blunt the effects of the initial disruption. Examples of resilient responses include using less electricity in production processes, substituting toward alternative power sources, making use of alternative means to generate power, rescheduling production, and increasing the relative importance of the aspect of a firm that does not use electricity to a large extent. One mapping of the authors' estimated coefficients to the two-digit NAICS level is reported in Table B.4.

Conceptually, the sector resilience coefficients can be interpreted as "scaling" the initial sectoral disruption (i.e., direct economic loss to a sector) to produce a shock that is more representative of the loss the industry is likely to experience, given its ability to attenuate some of the impacts. Following this logic, the coefficients can be incorporated into the I-O model in a straightforward manner. Recall from above that our core

---

19 Rose, Oladosu, and Liao, 2007.

20 Rose, Oladosu, and Liao, 2007, p. 517.

estimating framework is given by equation (15). When sector resilience is folded into the model, this becomes

$$\begin{bmatrix} \Delta x_1^R \\ \vdots \\ \Delta x_i^R \\ \vdots \\ \Delta x_n^R \end{bmatrix} = \begin{bmatrix} L_{1,1} \cdots L_{1,n} \\ \vdots \ \ddots \ \vdots \\ L_{n,1} \cdots L_{n,n} \end{bmatrix} \begin{bmatrix} 0 \\ \vdots \\ \Delta f_i \times R_i \\ \vdots \\ 0 \end{bmatrix}, \qquad (29)$$

$$\Delta \boldsymbol{x}^R = \boldsymbol{L} \Delta \boldsymbol{f}^R$$

where R_i denotes the resilience multiplier associated with sector i and variables containing a superscript "R" signify variables associated with a model that includes sector resilience. The sector resilience coefficients are multiplied by the presumed industry shocks (i.e., direct economic losses) to produce a transformed shock that is more representative of how much of the initial disruption each sector will ultimately absorb. As an example, suppose that Δf_i equals –\$100 and R_i equals 0.9, meaning that the product of the two equals –\$90. The refined model uses –\$90 as its initial disruption to industry i, reflecting the fact that inherent and adaptive responses by sector i are expected to reduce the direct economic loss it incurs by 10 percent.

This method of modeling sector resilience is promising but warrants caution. Rose, Oladosu, and Liao, 2007, estimates these multipliers in the specific context of a power outage in Los Angeles, and we utilized their estimates to illustrate our proposed sector resilience modeling strategy.[21] The coefficients are meant to capture how temporal substitution by industries allows them to blunt some of the impact of a disruption. However, sector resilience estimates may be sensitive to the estimation context. This can be seen by comparing the Rose, Oladosu, and Liao, 2007, estimates to others in the literature that were calculated in different settings.[22] For example, Canova, Coutinho, and Kontolemis, 2012, estimates sector resilience coefficients across European countries in the context of the 2008–2009 economic downturn; Klimek, Poledna, and Thurner, 2019, estimates sector resilience in response to economic shocks using a data set cover-

[21] Rose, Oladosu, and Liao, 2007.

[22] Fabio Canova, Leonor Coutinho, and Zenon Kontolemis, "Measuring the Macroeconomic Resilience of Industrial Sectors in the EU and Assessing the Role of Product Market Regulations," *European Economy Occasional Papers no. 112*, Brussels, Belgium: Directorate-General for Economic and Financial Affairs, 2012; Peter Klimek, Sebastian Poledna, and Stefan Thurner, "Quantifying Economic Resilience from Input-Output Susceptibility to Improve Predictions of Economic Growth and Recovery," *Nature Communications*, Vol. 10, No. 1677, 2019; Jacques Pelkmans, Lourdes Acedo, and Alessandro Maravalle, "How Product Market Reforms Lubricate Shock Adjustment in the Euro Area," *European Economy Economic Papers*, No. 341, 2008.

Table B.4
Rose, Oladosu, and Liao, 2007, Sector Resilience Coefficients

NAICS Two-Digit Code	Sector Title	Multiplier
11	Agriculture, Forestry, Fishing, and Hunting	0.024
21	Mining	0.732
22	Utilities	0.99
23	Construction	0.187
31–33	Manufacturing	0.712
42	Wholesale Trade	0.73
44–45	Retail Trade	0.661
48–49	Transportation and Warehousing	0.052
51	Information	0.7
52	Finance and Insurance	0.217
53	Real Estate Rental and Leasing	0.73
54	Professional, Scientific, and Technical Services	0.7
55	Management of Companies and Enterprises	0.70
56	Administrative, Support, Waste Management, and Remediation Services	0.691
61	Educational Services	0.542
62	Health Care and Social Assistance	0.427
71	Arts, Entertainment, and Recreation	0.57
72	Accommodation and Food Services	0.433
81	Other Services (except Public Administration)	0.691
92	Public Administration	0.05

ing 56 sectors and 43 countries between 2000 and 2014; and Pelkmans, Acedo, and Maravalle, 2008, estimates sector resilience in response to supply and demand shocks for 12 sectors in 11 Euro-area countries between 1970 and 2005. While some patterns emerge—certain industries tend to be more or less resilient than others—the magnitudes of the coefficients and the relative ranking of sectors by resilience can exhibit meaningful variability across scenarios.

If sector resilience estimates were calculated across a range of disaster scenarios, the sector resilience strategy may enable higher-quality I-O results. Such disaster scenarios could include hurricanes, floods, earthquakes, and tsunamis. If different series of estimates were constructed for different disaster scenarios, one could replace the variable R_i in equation (29) with a variable $R_{i,d}$, with d denoting the disaster scenario from which the estimates were derived. With this additional data, the approach detailed above would likely produce more realistic estimates for different disaster scenarios.

Capturing Downstream Economic Effects

Another drawback of the canonical I-O model is its inability to capture the "downstream" or "forward" supply chain effects that follow from an initial disruption to one or more sectors. As discussed earlier in this appendix, the I-O model only captures indirect economic effects through upstream linkages because of the nature of the technical coefficients matrix on which the estimates are based. To get a complete picture of the economic effects of disasters and disaster mitigation, both upstream and downstream effects should be accounted for to the extent possible. We propose using an approach similar to Ghosh, 1958, to approximate downstream effects in a straightforward, easily implementable manner. The discussion that follows draws on related material contained in Miller and Blair, 2009.

The Ghosh approach is methodologically similar to the Leontief I-O approach. The key distinction lies in the differing assumptions at the heart of each model. As noted previously in this appendix, the Leontief I-O model assumes that producers use inputs in fixed proportions. In contrast, the Ghosh approach assumes that sectors send fixed proportions of their output to those sectors that use it as a production input. This concept is represented by what are called *allocation coefficients* (analogous to the Leontief technical coefficients); allocation coefficients are formulated according to equation (30) below:

$$b_{i,j} = \frac{z_{i,j}}{x_i}. \tag{30}$$

They can be collected in an allocation matrix, $\boldsymbol{B}$, as follows:

$$\boldsymbol{B} = \begin{bmatrix} b_{1,1} \cdots b_{1,n} \\ \vdots \quad \ddots \quad \vdots \\ b_{n,1} \cdots b_{n,n} \end{bmatrix}. \tag{31}$$

Note that, in a sense, this amounts to "rotating" the Leontief I-O model. In Leontief's I-O model, we constructed the $\boldsymbol{A}$ matrix by dividing each element of $\boldsymbol{Z}$ by its corresponding column industry's total output. Here, we construct $\boldsymbol{B}$ by dividing each element of $\boldsymbol{Z}$ by its corresponding row industry's total output. This leads to a difference in interpretation of the two sets of coefficients; $b_{i,j}$ represents the proportion of industry i's total output that is sent to industry j to be used as a production input by industry j. As a consequence, this approach will only capture indirect economic effects related to "downstream" or "forward" supply chain linkages. As was the case for the technical coefficients, we assume that the allocation coefficients are fixed numbers that do not change. We can then express the value of total output as

$$\boldsymbol{x}^{D} = \boldsymbol{B}'\boldsymbol{x}^{D} + \boldsymbol{v}, \tag{32}$$

where the superscript "D" represents variables associated with a downstream economic effects model, $\boldsymbol{B}'$ denotes the transpose of $\boldsymbol{B}$, and $\boldsymbol{v}$ is a column vector containing total value-added expenditures by each sector.[23] In what follows, we replace $\boldsymbol{v}$ with $\boldsymbol{f}$ given the equivalence of the values of total value-added expenditures and total final demand at the regional level; this facilitates estimating upstream and downstream indirect economic effects using a common baseline.

We then solve the model using the same approach used to solve the Leontief I-O model; the solution is given by

$$\boldsymbol{x}^{D} = \left(\boldsymbol{I} - \boldsymbol{B}'\right)^{-1}\boldsymbol{f} = \boldsymbol{G}\boldsymbol{f}. \tag{33}$$

The expected total economic effects of an initial change in the final output of one or more sectors can then be calculated using equation (34) below:

$$\Delta\boldsymbol{x}^{D} = \boldsymbol{G}\Delta\boldsymbol{f}. \tag{34}$$

As was the case with the Leontief I-O model, subtracting $\Delta\boldsymbol{f}$ from $\Delta\boldsymbol{x}^{D}$ isolates the projected indirect economic effects, where here the indirect economic effects are only those associated with downstream repercussions. Again, this is a consequence of the structure of $\boldsymbol{B}$ and, hence, $\boldsymbol{G}$. Upon incorporating sector resilience into this model, we obtain our final downstream effects specification:

$$\begin{bmatrix} \Delta x_1 \\ \vdots \\ \Delta x_n \end{bmatrix} = \begin{bmatrix} G_{1,1} \cdots G_{1,n} \\ \vdots \quad \ddots \quad \vdots \\ G_{n,1} \cdots G_{n,n} \end{bmatrix} \begin{bmatrix} \Delta f_1 \times R_1 \\ \vdots \\ \Delta f_n \times R_n \end{bmatrix} = \boldsymbol{G}\Delta\boldsymbol{f}^{\mathrm{R}}. \tag{35}$$

Concluding Remarks

Given the recommended modifications to the traditional I-O model described above, we can now present the complete model for projecting the economic effects of pre-

[23] Conceptually, $\boldsymbol{x}^{D}$ is in fact the value of total outlays. When all inputs are accounted for, this equals the value of total output, which is why we have referred to $\boldsymbol{x}^{D}$ as the value of total output and maintained the corresponding notation.

Table B.5
Model Summary for Estimating the Economic Effects of Predisaster Mitigation

Component	Without Mitigation	With Mitigation	Value of Mitigation
Direct	$\Delta f^{R,N}$	$\Delta f^{R,Y}$	$\Delta f^{R,N} - \Delta f^{R,Y}$
Indirect (upstream)	$\Delta x^{R,U,N} - \Delta f^{R,N}$	$\Delta x^{R,U,Y} - \Delta f^{R,Y}$	$\left(\Delta x^{R,U,N} - \Delta f^{R,N}\right) - \left(\Delta x^{R,U,Y} - \Delta f^{R,Y}\right)$
Indirect (downstream)	$\Delta x^{R,D,N} - \Delta f^{R,N}$	$\Delta x^{R,D,Y} - \Delta f^{R,Y}$	$\left(\Delta x^{R,D,N} - \Delta f^{R,N}\right) - \left(\Delta x^{R,D,Y} - \Delta f^{R,Y}\right)$
Total indirect	$\Delta x^{R,U,N} + \Delta x^{R,D,N} - 2\Delta f^{R,N}$	$\Delta x^{R,U,Y} + \Delta x^{R,D,Y} - 2\Delta f^{R,Y}$	$\left(\Delta x^{R,U,N} + \Delta x^{R,D,N} - 2\Delta f^{R,N}\right) - \left(\Delta x^{R,U,Y} + \Delta x^{R,D,Y} - 2\Delta f^{R,Y}\right)$
Total effects	$\Delta x^{R,U,N} + \Delta x^{R,D,N} - \Delta f^{R,N}$	$\Delta x^{R,U,Y} + \Delta x^{R,D,Y} - \Delta f^{R,Y}$	$\left(\Delta x^{R,U,N} + \Delta x^{R,D,N} - \Delta f^{R,N}\right) - \left(\Delta x^{R,U,Y} + \Delta x^{R,D,Y} - \Delta f^{R,Y}\right)$

disaster mitigation efforts. Table B.5 illustrates how to use the model to compute these effects and partitions the total economic effects into its separate components: the direct economic effect, the indirect upstream economic effect, and the indirect downstream economic effect. The calculations described in the table will result in estimates for each industry; summing the estimates across industries produces estimates at the economy-wide level. Here, we denote with a superscript "U" variables associated with the Leontief I-O model to call attention to the fact that it is an upstream effects model and to differentiate it from the Ghosh model we have just described. Superscript "R" represents a variable associated with a model that incorporates sector resilience; superscript "D" denotes variables associated with the downstream effects model; superscript "N" designates variables corresponding to the scenario in which mitigation efforts did not occur prior to the disaster; and superscript "Y" signifies variables corresponding to the scenario in which mitigation efforts had taken place before the disaster.

The last topic for discussion is how to set the initial sectoral disruptions and sector recovery paths that the model requires. These can be computed in a number of ways, and optimal approaches vary according to context. In the context of the BRIC program, we recommend leveraging FEMA's Hazus tool to estimate both the initial sectoral disruptions and sector recovery paths following a disaster scenario. The initial sectoral disruption in the I-O model reflects the expected change in the value of a sector's production of final goods and services over a given time frame—in other words, business interruption losses. Hazus contains a direct economic loss module that estimates, by sector, business interruption losses, the dollar value of building-related direct economic losses, and lifeline infrastructure and transportation system direct economic losses for a host of disaster scenarios. The business interruption losses component of this module can thus be leveraged in an I-O model; there are also added benefits to using the Hazus estimates, such as maintaining consistency throughout the disaster planning process.

When translating the Hazus direct economic loss estimates into sectoral disruptions for indirect effects analysis, it is important to distinguish between stock measures versus flow measures. A stock quantity is measured at a point in time, whereas a flow quantity is measured over a given period. The I-O model is a flow model that estimates economic effects over a given time interval. Hence, care needs to be taken to ensure that the direct economic loss figures that are translated into this indirect effects model represent corresponding flow measures. For this reason, business interruption losses are the most appropriate measure to use as the direct economic effect component of the model. Damage to capital equipment or the building stock corresponds to effects on stock measures and hence should be avoided when estimating either model. Hazus also contains industry restoration functions, which capture the expected recovery path of each industry following a disruption. These can be used in conjunction with Hazus information on lifeline infrastructure recovery times and expenditures to create sector recovery paths for the I-O model.

Computable General Equilibrium Analysis for the Building Resilient Infrastructure and Community Program

Like I-O models, CGE models are economywide models. They estimate how economic actors—households, firms, and the government—interact with each other through supply and demand relationships. Both classes of models ultimately have the same objective: to estimate how changes in certain aspects of the economy affect the broader economy. Such changes may arise because of events like policy changes or natural disasters, which will affect output, prices, and economic incentives. Accordingly, the two sets of models rely on similar forms of data, require similar inputs, and produce similar outputs.

The primary difference lies in how economic interactions are modeled. CGE models are simulation-based optimization models. They simulate economies by optimizing the behavior of each economic actor given budget and resource constraints. For households, this means maximizing welfare (utility) by choosing what and how much to consume given the constraints imposed by income levels and taxation. For firms, this means maximizing profits by choosing amounts of capital, labor, and intermediate inputs subject to their respective prices and the limits of their production processes. The government is often relatively passive in these models, setting taxation levels and redistributing income according to the modeler's choices. Equilibrium in CGE models arises when economywide prices and quantities are such that all markets clear, and each segment of the economy is optimizing given the constraints it faces.

A key implication of this optimization-based structure is that CGE models estimate changes in prices and reactions to those changes. For households, changes in the relative prices of goods and services affect their income and optimal consumption profiles. For firms, price changes affect their chosen inputs to production—capital, labor, and intermediate goods and services—and, consequently, production levels. CGE models therefore contain rational economic behavior that ultimately serves to mitigate the economic effects of a disaster: when certain goods and services become relatively scarce, this affects relative prices, which, in turn, spurs households and firms to choose new optimal quantities of consumption, inputs, and outputs. Thus, this class of models is relatively better suited to estimating the effects of longer-term disruptions where such behavior is feasible, plausible, and an important driver of realized economic effects.

The way in which CGE models project the economic effects of disasters and disaster mitigation activities is conceptually similar to that of I-O models. First, the direct economic effects of a disaster on each sector are estimated. Next, CGE models simulate the resulting relative prices and quantities across markets that characterize the new economic equilibrium. The total and indirect economic effects of the disaster can then be inferred by comparing the initial and subsequent equilibria. Likewise, the projected economic benefits of disaster mitigation efforts are constructed by considering two different prospective before-and-after situations: (1) the economic changes following a disaster when no mitigation efforts occurred and (2) the economic changes following a disaster given that mitigation efforts did occur before the disaster hit. Comparing economic outcomes across these two scenarios yields the projected economic benefits of the mitigation efforts. If a CGE model is estimated using more granular SAM data, it can also project the economic effects of natural disasters and disaster mitigation on various socioeconomic groups because it explicitly models the household sector.

CGE models have their limitations, some of which are particularly relevant when estimating the indirect economic effects of a natural disaster where identifying the impacts immediately after the event is desirable. This is because CGE models assume that the economy returns to equilibrium, which would likely not happen immediately after the disaster. Without adjustment, the return-to-equilibrium assumption can produce a lower-bound estimate of economic impacts that can be misleading and show a deceivingly resilient postdisaster scenario.[24] Another limitation is the computational

[24] Albala-Bertrand, 2014; Rose and Gauri-Shankar Guha, 2004; Rose and Liao, 2005.

complexity of CGE models where computational constraints limit the number of sectors that can be included in the model.[25] Furthermore, failing to capture economic resilience can pose limitations to CGE estimates. Economic resilience occurs when economic actors substitute relatively scarce resources with something else (e.g., if the public water supply is disrupted, using bottled water). Firms can also make up lost income by overworking once the economy has started to recover.[26] Despite these limitations, Kajitani and Tatano's (2018) recent validation study shows that CGE estimates of the economic impacts from the 2011 earthquake and tsunami in Japan are consistent with observed production change in both directly and indirectly affected regions.[27]

The rest of this section proceeds as follows. First, we provide an in-depth treatment of a canonical CGE model used for natural hazard analysis. Next, we describe a set of options for employing a CGE model to support the BRIC program. Finally, we briefly discuss how to create an infrastructure to ease a possible transition from an I-O to CGE model for BRIC indirect benefits analysis.

Model Inputs and Data

The CGE framework requires two types of inputs. First, it requires data from an I-O or SAM table for the study region.[28] A SAM is an extended I-O table; in addition to industry-level data, it incorporates disaggregated institutional accounts for households and governments.[29] The CGE framework simulates the simultaneous optimizing behavior of economic actors, such as individual consumers, firms, and governments, using supply and demand functions subject to account balances and resource constraints. The data fed into these supply and demand functions come from I-O or SAM tables. The raw data provide a benchmark for the economy. Once an economic shock occurs from a natural hazard event, economic actors reoptimize and the difference between the old and new equilibria is used to estimate the impact that the natural hazard had on the economy.

Second, the CGE framework utilizes substitution elasticities. Common substitution elasticities used in CGE modeling are Armington elasticities between national and foreign goods, substitution elasticities between production sectors (such as capital and labor), and household substitution elasticities (such as those between consump-

---

[25] Marten and Garbaccio, 2018.

[26] Rose and Liao, 2005; Rose and Guha, 2004; Rose, Oladosu, and Liao, 2007.

[27] Kajitani and Tatano, 2017.

[28] Rose and Liao, 2005; Rose, Oladosu, and Liao, 2007; Adam Rose, Ian Su Wing, Dan Wei, and Misak Avetisyan, *Total Regional Economic Losses from Water Supply Disruptions to the Los Angeles County Economy*, final report to Los Angeles County Economic Development Corporation, USC, 2012; FEMA, *Multi-Hazard Loss Estimation Methodology, Flood Model, Hazus—MH Technical Manual*, undated c.

[29] FEMA, undated c.

tion and leisure).[30] The elasticities of substitution define how consumption and production inputs respond to changes in relative prices.

Canonical Computable General Equilibrium Model for Natural Hazard Analysis

Overview

A variety of studies have used the CGE framework to assess the economic impacts of a natural hazard.[31] We identify Marten and Garbaccio, 2018; Wing, Rose, and Wein, 2015; and Rose and Liao, 2005, as references of particular interest for BRIC. Marten and Garbaccio, 2018, exemplifies a general CGE model that can be applied to any region by characterizing the region of interest into a predetermined set of economies. Wing, Rose, and Wein, 2015, builds a CGE model for the California region that estimates the indirect economic loss from direct lifeline service outages. Rose and Liao, 2005, estimates the indirect economic loss to the Portland, Oregon, region from a water utility service outage after an earthquake. In this section, we use Adam Rose and Shu-Yi Liao's paper to discuss the CGE framework in further detail.

Rose and Liao, 2005

We focus on Rose and Liao's paper because of its relevance to the BRIC program. Additionally, their case study highlights the impacts to a lifeline service, which demonstrates the model's applicability to BRIC lifeline sector priorities. Rose and Liao's paper uses CGE methods to evaluate economic impacts in the context of an earthquake that causes a disruption to water utility services in the Portland, Oregon, metro area. The following discussion dissects Rose and Liao's approach. We then discuss the possibilities for tailoring Rose and Liao's model to the BRIC program.

Rose and Liao's paper advances CGE modeling in the natural hazard mitigation context by building a framework for specifying economic resilience and by decomposing direct and indirect effects through partial and general equilibrium responses. These advancements are particularly important to consider in the BRIC context. For instance, accounting for economic resilience when estimating the cost of a natural disaster helps deflate estimates that would otherwise not consider the choices economic actors can make in an emergency. In the water disruption case for instance, economic actors have adaptation options such as input substitution (e.g., importing water from surrounding regions or using bottled water) and conservation that can help avoid maximum potential loss. Rose and Liao incorporate this into their model by adjusting the substitution elasticity parameters for the production functions to measure adaptations that firms can take during emergencies. Moreover, Rose and Liao advance CGE modeling by using a novel method to decompose the indirect costs from the total costs

---

[30] Marten and Garbaccio, 2018.

[31] For example, Carrera et al., 2015; Chang, 2003; Rose and Guha, 2004; Marten and Garbaccio, 2018; Rose and Liao, 2005; Tatano and Tsuchiya, 2008; Wing, Rose, and Wein, 2015.

as a result of a natural hazard. Prior to their paper, the CGE framework estimated the total impact without any deconstruction to pinpoint direct versus indirect effects. Separating direct from indirect costs can provide more informative results, which can in turn provide more useful metrics to consider when evaluating prospective mitigation projects.

Rose and Liao apply their CGE framework to a hypothetical major earthquake disruption to the Portland Metropolitan Water System and analyze the resulting sectoral and regional economic impacts. The Portland case study is directly relevant to the BRIC context because it focuses on a disruption to a DHS-categorized lifeline service in a major metropolitan area and because it models the economic impacts both locally and regionally. The water and wastewater systems sector is a lifeline listed under DHS's 16 critical infrastructure sectors.[32] In the BRIC context, understanding the impacts that natural hazards can cause to lifeline critical infrastructures is important because these infrastructures are vital to security, health, and safety. Additionally, measuring the impacts to lifeline critical infrastructures shows that the economic cost to disasters can be large even when the cost to property damage is small or concentrated.[33]

Rose and Liao Computable General Equilibrium Model—Five Components

Rose and Liao's CGE model has five components: (1) production functions, (2) demand functions, (3) economic resilience measures, (4) model assumptions, and (5) indirect loss estimation. The production and demand components measure the interactions between the economic actors. The economic resilience component increases the precision of the production function by incorporating different responses firms can take in the wake of a hazard. The assumptions lay the groundwork on which the model works. The indirect losses are calculated by decomposing loss estimates through a three-step process. The following sections dive deeper into each of the five components in Rose and Liao's CGE model.

Production Functions

The production component is expressed by a multitiered constant elasticity of substitution (CES) production function. This system of equations represents a hierarchical decisionmaking process at the firm level. There are four equations in this system with five aggregate inputs to production: capital (assets such as infrastructure or machinery), labor, energy, materials, and water. For any given level of output, the model expresses how the firm chooses the combination of these five inputs that produces the desired level of output without overstepping cost constraints. The elasticities of substitution measure the firms' input choices by expressing how input proportions respond to prices. The multiple equations allow for the use of different substitution elasticities

[32] Cybersecurity and Infrastructure Security Agency, "Critical Infrastructure Sectors," webpage, last revised March 24, 2020.

[33] Rose and Liao, 2005.

for different pairs of inputs so that elasticities can vary across equations. The production function models the levels of production firms make given aggregate inputs, cost constraints, and elasticities of substitution.

Demand Functions

The demand component models the consumers in the economy: households and governments. Rose and Liao estimate the household demand for commodities and services using CES utility functions. Utility functions model consumer choice based on preferences and budgetary constraints. Rose and Liao estimate government demand for commodities and services from national account data fixed at their base-year level. Households are classified into three groups by income level, and government fiscal activity is divided at the federal, state, and local level.

Economic Resilience Levels

Rose and Liao's implementation of an economic resilience component in their CGE model was a contribution to the precision of CGE modeling in a natural hazard context. Economic resilience measures a firm's ability to adapt and respond to natural hazards in a way that increases avoided loss. For instance, firms can adapt in the aftermath of a natural hazard by skipping routine maintenance to use less resources, turning off unnecessary water facilities (such as fountains), reusing water, or conserving water. Additionally, firms can practice resilience by substituting other inputs for water systems through deliveries, by purchasing water from other sources, or by using a backup supply.

Rose and Liao implement three resilience metrics: conservation efforts, substitution efforts, and a combination of both conservation and substitution efforts. Resilience is measured in the model by the difference between (1) the I-O model's fixed coefficient production function, which yields an upper-bound estimate of direct output losses, and (2) the coefficient of the result from a production function, which captures the resilient response mechanisms. The coefficient from (2) is obtained by altering the elasticity parameters in the sectoral production functions of the CGE model. Recall that the elasticity of substitution parameters measure firm choices. In this case, this would be the choice of adapting water through conservation and/or substitution. Thus, deriving the elasticity parameter in the case that firms practice conservation and/or substitution efforts provides the model component necessary for measuring economic resilience.

Model Assumptions

Rose and Liao generally use three assumptions to build the framework for their CGE model. First, they assume that the market clearing and closure rules are such that for all commodity and service markets associated with the Portland region, associated with imports, and associated with exports, demand and supply are equated. Second, their model assumes that each sector has fixed capital stock. Finally, they balance the market using the Keynesian closure rule so that the labor market is balanced at under-employment. Relatedly, Rose and Liao assume mobile labor across the different sectors.

Indirect Loss

Indirect loss is the last component of Rose and Liao's CGE model. They calculate indirect loss using a three-step process that decomposes the loss estimates into two categories: direct and indirect. Direct loss is associated with the partial equilibrium solution and indirect loss is then calculated as the difference between total general and partial equilibrium using the following three-step process:

1. Extract the sectoral production functions from the CGE model, and adjust parameters and variables in them one at a time to match empirical direct loss estimates.
2. Reinsert the recalibrated sectoral production functions into the CGE model, reduce input supply to a level consistent with empirical estimates, and compute total regional losses.
3. Subtract direct losses from total losses to determine indirect losses.[34]

The partial equilibrium (direct effects) are estimated by modeling the supply and demand functions that use a subset of inputs to production as variables. These variables are often labor, capital, technology, and (in the case of hazard mitigation analysis) a lifeline utility sector such as water. The results are estimates based on changes for a subset of the market's inputs, holding all others constant. For instance, these results are the direct economic effects of an earthquake that damages water utility systems. In reality, a lot of other sectors are directly affected. These impacts can be modeled across the entire economy by using projected sector-level direct effects as inputs to the CGE model, which will then estimate the total general equilibrium of the postdisaster economy. One can then subtract the partial equilibrium (direct effects) from the total general equilibrium to estimate the indirect effects. As a result, the losses that occur as a result of ripple effects from the directly affected sectors are estimated.

Limitations

CGE models have their limitations, some of which are particularly concerning when estimating the indirect economic effects of a natural disaster where identifying the impacts immediately after the event is desirable. This is because CGE models assume that the economy returns to equilibrium, something that would likely not happen immediately after the disaster. Without adjustment, the return-to-equilibrium assumption can produce a lower-bound estimate of economic impacts that can be misleading and show a deceivingly resilient postdisaster scenario. The resulting uncertainties can be reconciled by understanding that the specific sectoral, industrial, and regional eco-

[34] Rose and Liao, 2005, p. 95.

nomic interactions improve on other methods and are crucial to consider when estimating indirect economic impacts.[35] Another limitation is the computational complexity of CGE models, where computational constraints limit the number of sectors that can be included in the model.[36] Furthermore, failing to capture economic resilience can pose limitations to CGE estimates. Economic resilience occurs when economic actors substitute lost resources with something else (e.g., if the public water supply is disrupted, using bottled water). Firms can also make up lost income by overworking once the economy has started to recover.[37] Despite these limitations, Kajitani and Tatano's (2018) recent validation study shows that CGE estimates of the economic impacts from the 2011 earthquake and tsunami in Japan are consistent with observed production change in both directly and indirectly impacted regions.[38]

Rose and Liao Case Study

Rose and Liao use a case study to apply their model in the event of a hypothetical earthquake disrupting water utility services in the Portland Oregon metro area. Portland Bureau of Water Works (PBWW) is a city-owned utility serving 840,000 people in 1998. The PBWW is rate financed and serves businesses that make up 98 percent and 72 percent of sales in two of the major counties in the Portland metro region. Major manufacturing companies, the Portland City Bureau of Parks and Recreation, and hospitals are the major customers of PBWW.

Rose and Liao adapt Adam Rose and his colleagues' (1997) methods that use a geographic information system overlay of employment data by workplace onto a water demand service area to crosswalk the water utility lifeline network to the regional economic model.[39] Rose and Liao use the 1998 IMPLAN SAM and I-O table for Multnomah and Washington Counties to model Portland's major economic actors using industry, commodity, factor income, households, government, capital, and trade accounts. The industry accounts are made up of 20 sectors,[40] with the water utility services separated from the other utility services so that the model estimates specifically the water supply disruptions from an earthquake disaster. The model is then run by

[35] Albala-Bertrand, 2014; Rose and Guha, 2004; Rose and Liao, 2005.

[36] Marten and Garbaccio, 2018.

[37] Rose and Liao, 2005; Rose and Guha, 2004; Rose, Oladosu, and Liao, 2007.

[38] Kajitani and Tatano, 2017.

[39] See also Stephanie E. Chang, "Evaluating Disaster Mitigations: Methodology for Urban Infrastructure Systems," *Natural Hazards Review*, Vol. 4, No. 4, 2003.

[40] The sectors include agriculture, mining, construction, food products, manufacturing, petroleum, transportation, communication, electric utilities, gas distribution, water and sanitary services, wholesale trade, retail trade, FIRE (finance, insurance, and real estate), personal services, business and professional services, entertainment services, health services, education services, and other services.

conducting simulations of the economy in the aftermath of an earthquake to estimate the regional economic impact because of a water supply disruption.

Model Outputs and Interpretation

The outputs of a CGE model show the estimated change in monetary value for each industry and economic actor account studied, expressed as total dollar amount or percentage change following a natural hazard event. Rose and Liao's outputs estimate the economic effects of a postdisaster water utility disruption through the percentage of total direct economic output losses, total direct output losses that account for economic resilience, indirect economic impacts, and total regional economic impacts. Summing the total changes across all industry accounts results in the total loss value or total percentage change in output, directly accounting for resilience, direct, and indirect economic losses.

CGE model outputs can be useful in a number of ways. First, the differences in losses between hazard mitigation activities and no hazard mitigation activities can be analyzed. The CGE model can be used to make these comparisons by replacing the disruption values because of expected damages with no mitigation activities with disruption values because of expected damages with predisaster mitigation activities. For instance, Rose and Liao run their CGE model estimating the effects of a water utility service disruption without mitigation and with cast-iron pipe replacement. Comparing the results between the two model runs provides evidence for the benefits of mitigation. For instance, Rose and Liao find that mitigation activities reduce the total direct water outage from 50.5 percent to 31 percent.

Second, CGE model outputs can be used to compare households by income when there are multiple household-level accounts that vary by income included in the baseline data. The results will show the direct and indirect economic losses to different households by income. Thus, one can analyze the differences in economic impact to households of different wealth levels with and without mitigation.[41]

Finally, the outputs can be used to compare industries and economic actors with one another and direct economic losses with indirect economic losses.[42] For instance, the output could be interpreted in such a way that shows that households at the lowest income level account for X percent of total indirect economic loss. Or the outputs could be interpreted to show that indirect economic losses account for Y percent of total economic losses. These three interpretation examples are not exhaustive, and CGE model outputs can be used to estimate other interesting issues such as economic resilience for the whole region and for individual economic actors.

---

[41] Marten and Garbaccio, 2018.

[42] Rose and Liao, 2005.

Options for Tailoring the Model to the Building Resilient Infrastructure and Community Program

CGE methods are complex, and there are many options for users to tailor their models to the issue they are studying. During CGE model development, for instance, users must make choices on what industries to disaggregate the economy to, what level of household characteristics to disaggregate consumers, how to measure government accounts, what data to use, what supply and demand functions to optimize, and how to calibrate the parameters to describe elasticity of substitution between economic actors. Thus, there is a menu of possible options for measuring indirect benefits using CGE methods. Three options should be considered: (1) building a general model, (2) following Rose and Liao's work to evaluate one critical lifeline sector, or (3) devoting special attention to multiple sectors simultaneously. The three options are listed in increasing order of complexity. The rest of this section discusses these three CGE modeling options in the BRIC context.

Option 1: Build a General Computable General Equilibrium Model

While CGE modeling is inherently complex, developing a general CGE model would be the relatively simplest option to pursue. A generalized model would choose the industry accounts, federal accounts, household accounts, and parameters from a predetermined set that depends on the size and type of the economy. Additionally, the appropriate supply and demand equations for each type of economy would need to be developed by modeling historic data from each of the economy types. The Environment Protection Agency (EPA), for instance, uses this approach to estimate the direct and indirect effects of environmental policies on the economy.[43] EPA's CGE model features nine regions with 23 sectors. The model characteristics of the nine regions vary to capture the different responses each region's economy might have a to a specific policy change.[44]

This general CGE model option could be implemented by asking grant applicants the appropriate questions to determine what type of economy each applicant falls under. The type of economy identified would then inform the appropriate predetermined economic accounts, parameters, and supply and demand equations to estimate the indirect economic losses from a natural hazard. The former default Hazus indirect economic loss module, for example, had 21 default economies that were determined by such characteristics as size, primary industry type, and unemployment rate.[45] BEA has economic account data and could be used as a source for each of the types of economies chosen in the general CGE model. However, the BEA data have their limitations. For instance, the household accounts are not differentiated by income level so differ-

[43] Marten and Garbaccio, 2018.

[44] Marten and Garbaccio, 2018.

[45] FEMA, undated c.

ences in effects across socioeconomic groups could not be evaluated.[46] EPA's regional model uses IMPLAN data, which can be used to analyze these types of heterogeneous effects. The general CGE model could then automatically calculate indirect economic effects after determining which general economy the applicant falls under.

Option 2: Follow Rose and Liao, 2005

The next option for consideration is a CGE model that follows Rose and Liao's analysis of a single critical sector. This option is more complex than a general CGE model because more refined data would be needed for the economy studied. Each regional economy has unique critical sectors and thus direct data from the region would be needed. Following Rose and Liao's CGE model would allow for analyzing the specific indirect effects of a natural hazard's disruption to lifeline assets, such as water, electricity, and transportation. Rose and Liao's model also enables hazard mitigation analysis by simulating the economy with and without mitigation efforts for a specific sector. This option requires more effort during the implementation phase because applicants would have to supply user-specific data. However, as a result, the estimates would be more precise and shed light on projected avoided loss to critical sectors.

Option 3: Devote Special Attention to Multiple Sectors Simultaneously

Taking Rose and Liao's model further by analyzing the indirect effects resulting from damage to multiple lifeline infrastructure sectors is a third option to consider. Wing, Rose, and Wein (2015) do this in the context of an atmospheric river event in California. They estimate the direct and indirect economic loss to California's economy using a CGE model that uses direct lifeline service outages for electricity, water, wastewater treatment, and telecommunications.[47] In addition to needing applicant-specific data for industry, government, and household accounts and parameters, the supply and demand optimization model would increase in complexity with the number of sectors studied. This would become computationally costly and implementation would rely on experts in CGE methods. Instead of a standardized model that could be used across many applicants, each applicant would have a unique model depending on their economy, their critical sectors, and the hazard studied. Although this model would create holistic estimates of indirect economic loss across all relevant critical sectors in the economy, the inaccessibility to applicants and computational burden would have to be taken into consideration.

---

[46] Bureau of Economic Analysis, 2013.

[47] Ian Wing, Adam Rose, and Anne Wein, "Economic Consequence Analysis of the ARkStorm Scenario," *Natural Hazards Review*, Vol. 17, 2015.

Transitioning from the Input-Output to a Computable General Equilibrium Model

In the case that an I-O model is developed to estimate the indirect benefits of hazard mitigation projects, much of that infrastructure could be leveraged during a transition to a CGE model. Recall that the CGE framework models a regional economy through supply and demand functions to estimate the monetary value of each of the economy's economic actors. The data used to model the supply and demand functions come from I-O or SAM accounts. To transition from I-O to CGE modeling in the context of BRIC, one would need to obtain SAM data (if they are deemed either necessary or preferable to BEA data), develop the supply and demand functions, derive the parameters, and model the economy.

SAMs provide additional information that further describes the study region's economy by including consumption, capital, and trade. The transfers are recorded at their origin, intermediary, and final destinations. The SAM framework also captures income generation through value-added accounts. Additionally, SAMs tend to include nonindustry accounts such as governments and households at different levels (e.g., state/federal and by income).[48] As previously discussed, the scope of acquiring SAM data would depend on the type of CGE model one decides to use. In the case of a general model, one could acquire the appropriate data for the different types of general economies identified through either IMPLAN or BEA. These data could either be acquired ex ante or provided by the applicant. Once the SAM data have been acquired, the next step is to develop the supply and demand functions.

The CGE model uses supply and demand functions to model the economy. These supply and demand functions will depend on the economy studied. The CGE model optimizes the behavior of economic actors, such as consumers, firms, and the government, subject to resource constraints such as income. The model runs its optimization algorithm over the supply and demand functions. These functions include production and demand components. These production and demand components will depend on the region economy studied. For example, Rose and Liao use a multitiered CES production function that represents a hierarchical decisionmaking process at the economic-actor level. In the case that a general CGE model is developed for different types of economies, these supply and demand functions would be tailored to each type of regional economy included. In the case that a sector-disruption-specific CGE model is developed, these functions will likely change depending on the region studied.

The last component of the CGE model is the elasticity parameters. The elasticity parameters measure substitution between sectors as a function of price changes. The elasticity parameters can be identified through mathematical derivations using the

[48] Jeffery Round, "Social Accounting Matrices and SAM-Based Multiplier Analysis," in F. Bourguignon and L. Pereira da Silva, eds., *The Impact of Economic Policies on Poverty and Income Distribution: Evaluation Techniques and Tools*, Washington, D.C.: World Bank, 2003.

supply and demand equations. Thus, they are region specific, and a model would need either preset elasticities for a set of general economies or they would have to be derived for each individual case, depending on the model that is chosen. Once the parameters have been established, the final step is to model the economy before and after a disruption using a program that calculates the economic accounts using a supply and demand optimization algorithm.

APPENDIX C

Applicant Institutional Capacity Insights from the International Development Literature

As described in Chapter Four, insights drawn from a convenience sample of academic and practitioner literature identified four key factors that contribute to government institutional capacity: (1) organization and procedures, (2) leadership, (3) a motivated and skilled workforce, and (4) material resources. Those factors and their relationship to AIC are discussed in Chapter Four.

Within this limited scope, HSOAC also identified several United Nations resources on institutional capacity. United Nations development programs have long experience supporting capacity-building efforts in lower-income countries. Their analyses and user guides identify key institutional performance factors and document lessons learned. Although public-sector organizations in lower-income countries may operate in more resource-constrained conditions than their developed-world counterparts, analyses drawn from their experience can help illuminate core characteristics of government institutional capacity across income and resource settings.

This appendix describes several frameworks and approaches for understanding institutional capacity that the HSOAC research team identified. These frameworks and approaches generally describe key elements of effective institutions and identify common capacity gaps and areas for improvement. We discuss them below.

The United Nations Development Programme

UNDP conducts capacity assessments using a structured methodology and a three-dimensional capacity assessment framework.[1] The three dimensions are (1) core issues, (2) functional and technical capacities, and (3) points of entry. The core issues dimension refers to four common capacity challenges: (1) institutional arrangements, (2) leadership, (3) knowledge, and (4) accountability. The functional and technical capacities dimension refers to the situation-specific range of competencies that a government

[1] United Nations Development Programme, *Capacity Assessment Methodology User's Guide*, New York, November 2008.

organization needs to achieve its goals and objectives. The points of entry dimension allows distinctions between capacity building at the individual, the organizational, and the environmental level. Together, the three dimensions provide an analytic framework for understanding capacity as a layered product of general organizational requirements and specific capabilities arranged across different levels of organization. The relationship is shown in Figure C.1.

In 2010, the UNDP Procurement Capacity Development Centre published a *Public Procurement Capacity Development Guide* that takes the UNDP capacity assessment framework as a starting point for designing national procurement system assessments.[2] The guide states that capacity assessments are iterative processes and lays out UNDP's five steps for conducting them: (1) engage stakeholders on capacity development; (2) assess capacity assets and needs; (3) formulate a capacity development

Figure C.1
United Nations Development Programme Capacity Assessment Framework

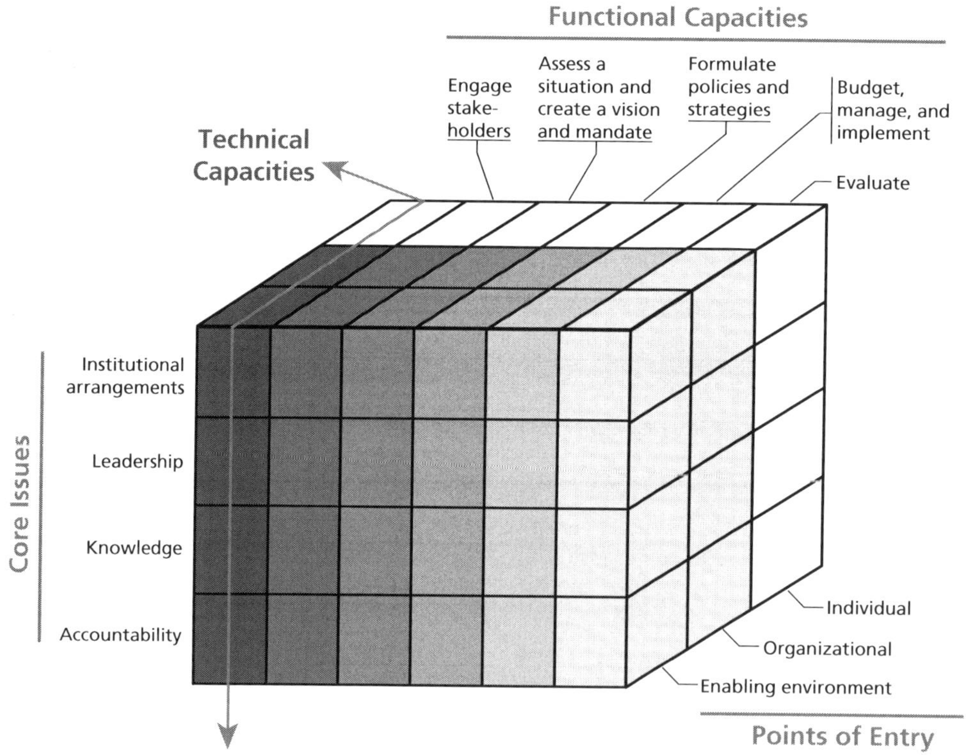

SOURCE: United Nations Development Programme, 2008

[2] Procurement Capacity Development Centre, Capacity Development Group, Bureau for Development Policy, United Nations Development Fund, *Public Procurement Capacity Development Guide*, New York, October 2010.

response; (4) implement a capacity development response; and (5) evaluate capacity development (Figure C.2). The guide follows the UNDP model by recognizing that capacity can be measured on three levels—the individual, the organizational, and the enabling environment—and that the four most common capacity issues involve institutional arrangements, leadership, knowledge, and accountability. The guide emphasizes that capacity assessments should be flexible and adaptive. Local stakeholders and clients should be consulted to understand what types of capacity are required by the agency in question and to understand who its target beneficiaries are. This helps to narrow the scope of capacity assessments, reducing resource requirements and maintaining focus on mission-essential capacities. The guide also describes the many types of information and data sources that can be used for capacity assessments, ranging from document reviews, questionnaires, and client satisfaction surveys to workshops, focus groups, and interviews.

The United Nations Capital Development Fund

The United Nations Capital Development Fund (UNCDF) has examined how to improve local institutional capacity so that local governments can be more effective

Figure C.2
United Nations Development Programme Capacity Development Process

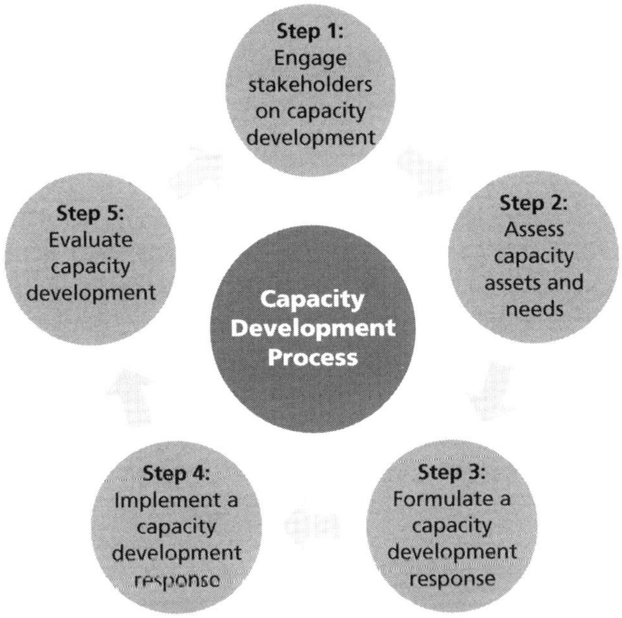

SOURCE: Procurement Capacity Development Centre, 2010.

partners in implementing the Millennium Development Goals.[3] UNCDF operates Local Development Programmes in many less-developed countries that seek to build "more effective, efficient, equitable, and accountable infrastructure and service delivery through rural local governments."[4] Based on Local Development Programme experience, UNCDF identified four common constraints on local government performance: (1) human resource constraints, (2) material and logistical constraints, (3) institutional constraints, and (4) performance incentivization constraints. Examples of human resource constraints include the lack of key personnel and skill sets, as well as a lack of employee understanding about institutional reform initiatives.[5] Some proposed interventions to improve human resources capacity are tying external funding to filling critical personnel gaps and developing additional guidelines and reference materials.

Material and logistical constraints arise from inadequate operating budgets or other resource limitations. UNCDF recommends that external partners consider targeted, "technically appropriate" support and pathways toward "sustainable mechanisms" for funding key expenses to address this type of constraint. Organizational policies and procedures that are "inappropriate" or "vague" and that undermine employee performance are given as examples of institutional constraints. UNCDF recommends developing more detailed and relevant procedures and reference materials, in addition to training employees in navigating new systems. Finally, incentive constraints arise when employee motivation and discipline are undermined by a lack of accountability and oversight. Recommendations to address incentives constraints include conditioning funding on program performance and pursuing legal, policy, or regulatory reforms.

Other practitioner-oriented international development resources take a similar approach by identifying gaps that must be addressed to build governmental institutional capacity. A Brookings Institution policy brief noted that limited institutional capacity in developing countries hampers the ability of aid recipients to absorb external resources and use them effectively.[6] The author found that institutional capacity-building efforts are linked to a wide range of governmental functions, ranging from law enforcement and regulatory oversight to the provision of public goods and services. Three types of "institutional malfunction" that hinder capacity building are resource-related malfunction, political-driven malfunction, and organizational malfunction.[7] Resource-related malfunctions stem from "chronic congestion," when demand for government services outpaces supply; from "inadequate input," when there is a lack of

[3] United Nations Capital Development Fund, *Delivering the Goods: Building Local Government Capacity to Achieve the Millennium Development Goals*, New York, June 2007.

[4] United Nations Capital Development Fund, 2007.

[5] United Nations Capital Development Fund, 2007.

[6] Carol Graham, *Strengthening Institutional Capacity in Poor Countries*, Washington, D.C.: Brookings Institution, April 2002.

[7] Graham, 2002.

appropriately skilled workers or other resources; or from monopolization of funding by personnel costs.[8] Political-driven institutional malfunctions result from corruption, politicization, or special interest capture. Sources of organizational institutional malfunctions include ambiguity about an organization's goals, fluctuating institutional priorities, and too much or too little involvement by government agencies with management or oversight responsibilities.

U.S. Agency for International Development

The HSOAC review team identified a USAID Human and Institutional Capacity Development (HICD) model designed to diagnose and address the root causes of performance gaps in organizations of all types.[9] The USAID HICD handbook considers organizations to be "adaptive systems" with "interrelated functions" that must continually adjust to changes in their environment.[10]

The HICD approach compares an organization's real-world performance with what it should be capable of achieving. The performance gap between the real and the potential performance state is then traced to shortcomings in one or more of six key performance factors. Targeted performance gap findings are then used to identify performance solutions. The six key performance factors are (1) information (clear expectations, regular feedback, etc.); (2) resources and tools (necessary materials and expert support, a safe and appropriate work environment); (3) incentives (financial and nonfinancial incentives, fulfilling jobs, a positive work environment); (4) knowledge and skills (employee knowledge, skills, and training); (5) motives (employee motivation); and (6) capacity (requirements-based recruitment and employee capacity to learn tasks).

---

[8] Graham, 2002.

[9] U.S. Agency for International Development, *Human and Institutional Capacity Development Handbook*, August 2011.

[10] U.S. Agency for International Development, 2011.

APPENDIX D

Applicant Institutional Capacity Interview Protocol

Introduction Script

Thank you for taking the time to speak with me today. Before we begin our session, I'd like to briefly tell you a bit about the project and how this discussion will be used.

Our team is affiliated with HSOAC, which is one of DHS's federally funded research and development centers. FEMA has engaged our team to conduct research on behalf of a hazard mitigation grant program. As part of that research, we are working to understand how different factors may affect the program's ability to lower future DRF response and recovery costs by spending money on mitigation now. One of these factors is *applicant institutional capacity*, or AIC.

AIC is an applicant's ability to plan high-quality mitigation projects and execute those projects effectively, especially in terms of completing projects on time and on budget. When an applicant has cost and schedule overruns, the project provides less mitigation benefit than it would have otherwise.

A number of institutional capacity factors affect applicant performance. Our team needs to understand what and how factors influence applicant institutional capacity so that we can provide recommendations on how to identify and manage AIC-based risk.

You have been identified as a FEMA subject-matter expert with knowledge that can support informed judgment and prediction on the issue of applicant institutional capacity. Soon, we will begin our session that will last about 90 minutes. I'll ask you a variety of questions to identify factors that influence applicant institutional capacity and how these factors influence the likelihood of staying *on budget* and likelihood of completing projects *on time*. Please try to answer them as best you can. I will ask questions in a particular order to minimize known biases, and I may at times ask follow-up questions to be sure I understand. We only have a short amount of time, so I may read off a script at times to make sure we stay on task and get the most useful information.

A member of our team will be taking notes about our conversation today. No one outside of the project team will have access to the notes. We may use your insights from this session in our briefings or reports. However, we will only quote your wording directly or use your name if you specifically request that. Otherwise, we do not report to FEMA on what you said, because we want you to feel free to be candid with us. We also do not report on who completes the interview session. You are free to skip any question you do not want to answer, and you can stop participation in this session at any time.

My supervisor is Josh Mendelsohn. If you have any comments or concerns following this interview, you can email him at joshua_mendelsohn@rand.org or call him at 703-413-1100.

Before we begin, do you have any questions?

Let's get started.

Question	Probes
Background	
B1. Tell me a little bit about how your role (current or former) relates to the predisaster mitigation grant process.	• What are/were your responsibilities in the grant process? • What decisions do/did you make in the grant process? • How do/did you make those decisions? – Who else is/was involved in this decision-making? How are/were they involved? – What information do/did you receive to help make those decisions? – Are/Were there constraints that currently make these decisions more challenging? – Are/Were there enablers that make them easier? • Once you have made these decisions, how is/was that decision used? • Who do/did you provide information to regarding these decisions and why? • How do/did these decisions affect your organization/ other organizations?
Evaluation of Applicant/Project Performance	
P1. What does/did successful project completion mean within your role?	• What factors, conditions or circumstances influence successful project completion? – Success to whom? • What factors affect *on-time* project completion? – What is the strength of this influence, in both positive and negative terms? • What factors affect *on-budget* project completion? – What is the strength of this influence, in both positive and negative terms?

Question	Probes
P2. What traits do successful applicants possess based on your current or former experience?	• What other factors could contribute to an applicant's success or failure? • What constrains the applicant's success? • Are there enablers that make a successful application more likely? – Are there ways to leverage these enablers? • Are there inhibiters that make a successful application less likely? – Are there ways to control for or limit the influence of theses inhibiters? • How can these traits be measured?
P3. How could applicants improve their likelihood of success?	• Why would these changes/traits/characteristics create a better success rate?
Evaluation of Applicant Capacity	
C1. Sometimes, projects are not on time or on budget because of factors outside the applicant's control, regardless of capacity. When this is the case, what factors are typically involved?	• How much do these factors influence project completion on time and on budget?
C2. What are the most important factors that influence an applicant's capacity to complete projects *on time*?	• What combination of factors make *on-time* project completion more/less likely, given your knowledge and experience? • Do these factors differ in any way for planning grants versus project grants?
C3. What are the most important factors that influence an applicant's capacity to complete projects *on budget*?	• What combination of factors make *on-budget* project completion more/less likely, given your knowledge and experience? • Do these factors differ in any way for planning grants versus project grants?
C4. How important are factors outside applicant control, such as unpredictable local conditions?	• Which factors are more influential? • Less?
If these factors are not mentioned, ask about them specifically	
X1. What influence does prior experience with hazard mitigation grants have on project performance?	• How important is this factor to project performance? • Does this factor differ in any way for planning grants versus project grants? • What are the benefits and risks associated with this factor?
X2. What influence does the size and capacity of an applicant's State Hazard Mitigation Office have on project performance?	• How important is this factor to project performance? • Does this factor differ in any way for planning grants versus project grants? • What are the benefits and risks associated with this factor?

Question	Probes
X3. What influence does how quickly mitigation funds are dispersed have on applicant project performance?	• How important is this factor to project performance? • Does this factor differ in any way for planning grants versus project grants? • What are the benefits and risks associated with this factor?
X4. What influence does leadership and quality of management have on project performance?	• How important is this factor to project performance? • Does this factor differ in any way for planning grants versus project grants? • What are the benefits and risks associated with this factor? • Probes: management continuity, program oversight, strategic vision
X5. What influence do material resources have on project performance?	• How important is this factor to project performance? • Does this factor differ in any way for planning grants versus project grants? • What are the benefits and risks associated with this factor? • Probes: funds, equipment, facilities
X6. What influence do organizational systems and structure, like transparent procedures and clear roles and responsibilities, have on project performance?	• How important is this factor to project performance? • Does this factor differ in any way for planning grants versus project grants? • What are the benefits and risks associated with this factor? • Probes: accounting, budgeting, and administrative systems, anticorruption controls
X7. What influence do workforce skills and training have on project performance?	• How important is this factor to project performance? • Does this factor differ in any way for planning grants versus project grants? • What are the benefits and risks associated with this factor? • Probes: workforce experience, education, motivation, incentives

APPENDIX E

Applicant Institutional Capacity Analysis Codebook

Codes	Definitions
Factors	
Internal	Factors that are internal to the applicant
a) Staff	Related to manpower/personnel
a. Quantity	Number of staff members/labor hours
b. Retention	Related to continued employment or staff turnover
c. Motivation	Staff enthusiasm, commitment, and initiative
d. Skill	Related to mitigation training and skill sets
e. Expertise	Dedicated staff with mitigation focus or expertise
b) Experience	Level of experience or institutional knowledge with mitigation grants
c) Leadership	Leadership and management qualities
d) Capability	Factors related to capability in performing successful projects
f. Management	Grant administration, project monitoring, the ability to manage grant implementation
g. Writing	Capacity for planning, developing, and writing grants
h. Technical	Engineering, benefit-cost analysis, time and cost estimation, attorneys, notaries and other technical expertise
i. Knowledge	Shrewd or savvy navigation of the grant program and/or its processes
j. Budget	Financial systems and controls and accounting
e) Resources	Availability of what is needed, when it's needed
a. Material	Computers, office equipment, other hardware, etc.
f) Organization	Related to clarity/transparency of roles, responsibilities, and procedures
g) Flexibility	Ability to be flexible as grant programs or circumstances change
h) Communication	Ability to communicate well within an organization

Codes	Definitions
External	Factors that are external to the applicant
a) Weather/climate	Weather or climate factors (e.g., rain or harsh winter conditions)
b) Disasters	Refers to any disaster activity and subsequent disruption
c) Processes	Refers to processes outside of the applicant's control in general
a. Requirements	Related to requirements such as environmental or historic preservation
b. Complexity	Red tape, paperwork, complicated or burdensome reporting requirements
c. Timeliness	Speed of funding disbursements, FEMA delays
d) Resources	Availability of what is needed, when it's needed
a. Material	Availability of supplies, material, contractors
b. Financial	Nonfederal cost share
c. Tools	Appropriate training, guidance, tools, checklists, etc.
e) Economic	Price changes, inflation, or other market conditions
f) Partnership	Support and relationships with state, local community, other stakeholders
g) Politics	Support from political leaders
h) Community traits	Characteristics of surrounding community (e.g., tax base, population size, income level)
i) Incentives	Performance-based incentives to improve applications or project performance
Between	
a) Communication	Between local, state, and federal
a. Top down	Related to communications from feds
b. Bottom up	Related to communications from states/locals
Suggestions	
Success	Related to how project/application success is/should/could be measured
Capacity	Related to how applicant capacity is/should/could be measured
Improvement	Related to suggestions/ideas on improving capacity or capability
a) Training	Increasing or improving training for better project performance or greater applicant capacity

Codes	Definitions
Levels	
Tribal	Related to tribes
Local	Related to local governments or subrecipients
State	Related to states
Federal	Related to the federal government/FEMA
Unit of analysis	
Project	Related to project success/completion, etc.
Applicant	Related to applicant capacity/success, etc.
Descriptors	
High	Block text related to or characteristic of high capacity
Low	Block text related to or characteristic of low capacity
On time	Block text related to or characteristic of on-time project completion
On budget	Block text related to or characteristic of on-budget project completion
Success	
Compliance	Staying within requirements
Impact	Demonstrated mitigation value
On budget	Completing within budget
On time	Completing within period of performance
Scope	Completing what you said you would
Work quality	Quality of the application or project work
Experience	**Refers to the interviewee's experience**
Nonfed	Includes tribal, local, or state experience
Fed only	Federal experience only
Position	**Refers to the interviewee's current professional position**
State Hazard Mitigation Office	
Planning	**Related to planning grants**

References

Adger, W. Neil, "Vulnerability," *Global Environmental Change*, Vol. 16, 2006, pp. 268–281.

Adger, W. Neil, Suraje Dessai, Marisa Goulden, Mike Hulme, Irene Lorenzoni, Donald R. Nelson, Lars Otto Naess, Johanna Wolf, and Anita Wreford, "Are There Social Limits to Adaptation to Climate Change?" *Climatic Change*, Vol. 93, 2009, pp. 335–354.

Albala-Bertrand, J. M., *Disasters and the Networked Economy*, Oxon, UK: Routledge, 2014.

Aubrecht, C., and D. Ozceylan, "Identification of Heat Risk Patterns in the U.S. National Capital Region by Integrating Heat Stress and Related Vulnerability," *Environment International*, Vol. 56, 2013, pp. 65–77.

Bakkensen, Laura A., Cate Fox-Lent, Laura K. Read, and Igor Linkov, "Validating Resilience and Vulnerability Indices in the Context of Natural Disasters," *Risk Analysis*, Vol. 37, No. 5, 2017, pp. 982–1004.

Balica, S., I. Popescu, L. Beevers, and N. Wright, "Parametric and Physically Based Modelling Techniques for Flood Risk and Vulnerability Assessment: A Comparison," *Environmental Modelling and Software*, Vol. 41, 2013, pp. 84–92.

Balica, S., N. Wright, and F. Van Der Meulen, "A Flood Vulnerability Index for Coastal Cities and Its Use in Assessing Climate Change Impacts," *Natural Hazards Review*, Vol. 64, 2012, pp. 73–105.

Berkeley Building Resilient Regions, Resilience Capacity Index, 2015. As of June 15, 2020: brr.berkeley.edu/rci/

Bess, Rebecca, and Zoe O. Ambargis, "Input-Output Models for Impact Analysis: Suggestions for Practitioners Using RIMS II Multipliers," paper presented at the 50th Southern Regional Science Association Conference, New Orleans, La., 2011. As of June 15, 2020:
https://www.bea.gov/research/papers/2011/
input-output-models-impact-analysis-suggestions-practitioners-using-rims-ii

Blessing, Russell, Samuel D. Brody, and Wesley E. Highfield, Valuing Floodplain Protection and Avoidance in a Coastal Watershed," *Disasters*, Vol. 43, No. 4, 2019, pp. 906–925.

Bond, Craig A., Aaron Strong, Nicholas Burger, Sarah Weiland, Uzaib Saya, and Anita Chandra, *Resilience Dividend Valuation Model: Framework Development and Initial Case Studies*, Santa Monica, Calif.: RAND Corporation, RR-2129-RF, 2017. As of June 15, 2020:
https://www.rand.org/pubs/research_reports/RR2129.html

Bradford, K., L. Abrahams, M. Hegglin, and K. Klima, "A Heat Vulnerability Index and Adaptation Solutions for Pittsburgh, Pennsylvania," *Environmental Science and Technology*, Vol. 49, No. 19, 2015, pp. 11303–11311.

Bullard, Clark W., and Anthony V. Sebald, "Monte Carlo Sensitivity Analysis of Input-Output Models," *Review of Economics and Statistics*, Vol. 70, No. 4, pp. 708–712.

Bureau of Economic Analysis, RIMS II: An *Essential Tool* for *Regional Developers* and *Planners*, Washington, D.C.: U.S. Department of Commerce, 2013. As of May 22, 2020:
https://www.bea.gov/sites/default/files/methodologies/RIMSII_User_Guide.pdf

Canova, Fabio, Leonor Coutinho, and Zenon Kontolemis, "Measuring the Macroeconomic Resilience of Industrial Sectors in the EU and Assessing the Role of Product Market Regulations," *European Economy Occasional Papers no. 112*, Brussels, Belgium: Directorate-General for Economic and Financial Affairs, 2012. As of June 15, 2020:
https://ec.europa.eu/economy_finance/publications/occasional_paper/2012/pdf/ocp112_en.pdf

Carrera, Lorenzo, Gabriele Standardi, Francesco Bosello, and Jaroslav Mysiak, "Assessing Direct and Indirect Economic Impacts of a Flood Event Through the Integration of Spatial and Computable General Equilibrium Modelling," *Environmental Modelling and Software*, Vol. 63, 2015, pp. 109–122. As of June 15, 2020:
https://doi.org/10.1016/j.envsoft.2014.09.016

Chang, Stephanie E., "Evaluating Disaster Mitigations: Methodology for Urban Infrastructure Systems," *Natural Hazards Review*, Vol. 4, No. 4, 2003, pp. 186–196.

Coughlin, Cletus, and Thomas B. Mandelbaum, "A Consumer's Guide to Regional Economic Multipliers," *Federal Reserve Bank of St. Louis Review*, Vol. 73, No. 1, January/February 1991, pp. 19–2.

Cutter, S. L., B. J. Boruff, and L. W. Shirley, "Social Vulnerability to Environmental Hazards," *Social Science Quarterly*, Vol. 84, No. 2, 2003, pp. 242–261.

Cutter, Susan L., Christopher G. Burton, and Christopher T. Emrich, "Disaster Resilience Indicators for Benchmarking Baseline Conditions," *Journal of Homeland Security and Emergency Management*, Vol. 7, No. 1, 2010. As of June 15, 2020:
https://doi.org/10.2202/1547-7355.1732

Cybersecurity and Infrastructure Security Agency, "Critical Infrastructure Sectors," webpage, last revised March 24, 2020. As of May 22, 2020:
https://www.cisa.gov/critical-infrastructure-sectors

Doherty, M., K. Klima, and J. Hellmann, "Climate Change in the Urban Environment: Advancing, Measuring, and Achieving Resiliency," *Environmental Science and Policy*, Vol. 66, 2016, pp. 310–313. As of June 15, 2020:
https://doi.org/10.1016/j.envsci.2016.09.001

Dwyer, Jody, *The ISO Building Code Effectiveness Grading Schedule*, MTAS Publications: Full Publications, 2012. As of June 15, 2020:
http://trace.tennessee.edu/utk_mtaspubs/163

Edgemon, Lesley, Carol Freeman, Carmella Burdi, John Hutchison, Karen Marsh, and Kyle Pfeiffer, *Community Resilience Indicator Analysis: County-Level Analysis of Commonly Used Indicators from Peer-Reviewed Research, 2019 Update*, Washington, D.C.: U.S. Department of Homeland Security, 2019. As of June 15, 2020:
https://www.fema.gov/media-library-data/1574791929443-de79e45eb04a7176570c3f6ec05e61a1/CRIA_2019_Update_508c_FINAL.pdf

Fekete, A., "Validation of a Social Vulnerability Index in Context to River-Floods in Germany," *Natural Hazards and Earth System Science*, Vol. 9, 2009, pp. 393–403.

Federal Emergency Management Agency, *FEMA's National Risk Index*, Washington, D.C.: FEMA, undated a. As of June 15, 2020:
https://proceedings.esri.com/library/userconf/proc17/papers/1837_145.pdf

———, "Glossary," webpage, undated b. As of May 22, 2020:
https://emilms.fema.gov/IS321/glossary.htm

———, *Multi-Hazard Loss Estimation Methodology, Flood Model, Hazus—MH Technical Manual*, undated c. As of May 22, 2020:
https://www.fema.gov/media-library-data/20130726-1820-25045-8292/hzmh2_1_fl_tm.pdf

———, "Public Assistance Funded Projects Detail," webpage, undated d. As of June 15, 2020:
https://www.fema.gov/data-sets

———, "Public Assistance Funded Projects Summary," webpage, undated e. As of June 15, 2020:
https://www.fema.gov/data-sets

———, *National Flood Insurance Program Community Rating System Coordinator's Manual*, FEMA FIA-15/2017, Washington, D.C.: FEMA, 2017. As of June 15, 2020:
https://www.fema.gov/media-library-data/1493905477815-d794671adeed5beab6a6304d8ba0b207/633300_2017_CRS_Coordinators_Manual_508.pdf

———, *National Flood Insurance Program Community Rating System: A Local Official's Guide to Saving Lives, Preventing Property Damage, and Reducing the Cost of Flood Insurance*, Washington, D.C.: FEMA, 2018. As of May 19, 2020:
https://www.fema.gov/media-library-data/1562876385763-262f88e35f4dde1484be9093b099e670/2018_NFIP_CRS_Brochure_June_2018_508OK_corrected.pdf

———, "OpenFEMA Data Repository," webpage, last updated October 15, 2018. As of June 15, 2020:
https://www.fema.gov/openfema

———, *E/L 0276 Benefit-Cost Analysis Training Student Manual*, Washington, D.C.: FEMA, June 2019a. As of June 15, 2020:
https://www.fema.gov/media-library-data/1567807912541-5a09d88f06245b28b5559e6255dcfddf/E-L_0276_Benefit-Cost_Analysis_Training_Student_Manual.zip

———, "Webinar Series 2019: Building Resilient Infrastructure and Communities," webpage, last updated August 22, 2019b. As of April 14, 2020:
https://www.fema.gov/drra-bric

———, "Community Resilience Indicator Analysis: County-Level Analysis of Commonly Used Indicators from Peer Reviewed Research," November 2019c. As of May 20, 2020:
https://www.fema.gov/media-library/assets/documents/176618.

———, "Benefit-Cost Analysis," webpage, last updated February 14, 2020a. As of May 20, 2020:
https://www.fema.gov/benefit-cost-analysis

———, "Hazus in Detail," webpage, last updated May 22, 2020b. As of July 1, 2020:
https://www.fema.gov/hazus-detail

FEMA—*see* Federal Emergency Management Agency

Fernandez, P., S. Mourato, M. Moreira, and L. Pereira, "A New Approach for Computing a Flood Vulnerability Index Using Cluster Analysis," *Physics and Chemistry of the Earth*, Vol. 94, 2016, pp. 47–55.

Flanagan, B., E. Gregory, E. Hallisey, J. Heitgerd, and B. Lewis, "A Social Vulnerability Index for Disaster Management," *Journal of Homeland Security and Emergency Management*, Vol. 8, No. 1, 2011. As of June 15, 2020:
https://doi.org/10.2202/1547-7355.1792

Foster, K., "In Search of Regional Resilience," in M. Weir, H. Wial, and H. Wolman, eds., *Building Regional Resilience: Urban and Regional Policy and Its Effects, Vol. 4*, Washington, D.C.: Brookings Institution, 2012, pp. 24–59.

Ghosh, Ambica, 1958. "Input-Output Approach in an Allocation System," *Economica*, Vol. 25, No. 97, 1958, pp. 58–64.

Giupponi, C., S. Giove, and V. Giannini, "A Dynamic Assessment Tool for Exploring and Communicating Vulnerability to Floods and Climate Change," *Environmental Modelling and Software*, Vol. 44, 2013, pp. 136–147.

Graham, Carol, *Strengthening Institutional Capacity in Poor Countries*. Brookings Institution, Washington, D.C.: Brookings Institution, April 2002. As of November 26, 2019:
https://www.brookings.edu/research/strengthening-institutional-capacity-in-poor-countries-shoring-up-institutions-reducing-global-poverty/

Greenberg, Michael R., Michael Lahr, and Nancy Mantell, "Understanding the Economic Costs and Benefits of Catastrophes and Their Aftermath: A Review and Suggestions for the U.S. Federal Government," *Risk Analysis*, Vol. 27, No. 1, 2007, pp. 83–96.

Haimes, Yacov Y., Barry M. Horowitz, James H. Lambert, Joost R. Santos, Chenyang Lian, and Kenneth G. Crowther, "Inoperability Input-Output Model for Interdependent Infrastructure Sectors. I: Theory and Methodology," *Journal of Infrastructure Systems*, Vol. 11, No. 2, 2005a, pp. 67–79.

———, "Inoperability Input-Output Model for Interdependent Infrastructure Sectors. II: Case Studies," *Journal of Infrastructure Systems*, Vol. 11, No. 2, 2005b, pp. 80–92.

Hall, Jeremy L., "Assessing Local Capacity for Federal Grant Getting," *American Review of Public Administration*, Vol. 38, No. 4, December 2008, pp. 463–479.

Hallisey, Elaine J., "Measuring Community Vulnerability to Natural and Anthropogenic Hazards: The Centers for Disease Control and Prevention's Social Vulnerability Index," *Journal of Environmental Health*, Vol. 80, No. 10, 2018, pp. 34–36.

Hondula, D. M., R. E. Davis, M. J. Leisten, M. V. Saha, L. M. Veazey, and C. R. Wegner, "Fine-Scale Spatial Variability of Heat-Related Mortality in Philadelphia County, USA, from 1983–2008: A Case-Series Analysis," *Environmental Health*, Vol. 11, 2012. As of June 15, 2020:
https://ehjournal.biomedcentral.com/articles/10.1186/1476-069X-11-16

IBHS—see Insurance Institute for Business and Home Safety.

IMPLAN, "Introducing the SAM," webpage, undated. As of June 15, 2020:
https://implanhelp.zendesk.com/hc/en-us/articles/115009674708-Introducing-the-SAM-

Insurance Institute for Business and Home Safety, "Disaster Safety," undated. As of May 21, 2020:
https://disastersafety.org/

Jun, K.-S., E.-S. Chung, E.-S., Y.-G. Kim, and Y. Kim, "A Fuzzy Multi-Criteria Approach to Flood Risk Vulnerability in South Korea by Considering Climate Change Impacts," *Expert Systems with Applications*, Vol. 40, No. 4, 2013, pp. 1003–1013.

Kajitani, Yoshio, and Hirokazu Tatano, "Applicability of a Spatial Computable General Equilibrium Model to Assess the Short-Term Economic Impact of Natural Disasters," *Economic Systems Research*, Vol. 30, 2017, pp. 1–24. As of June 15, 2020:
https://doi.org/10.1080/09535314.2017.1369010

Kiefer, John J., Monica T. Farris, and Natalie Durel, "Building Internal Capacity for Community Disaster Resiliency by Using a Collaborative Approach: A Case Study of the University of New Orleans Disaster Resistant University Project," *Journal of Emergency Management*, Vol. 4, No. 2, March/April 2006, pp. 24–28.

Klima, K., L. El Gammal, W. D. Kong, and D. Prosdocimi, "Creating a Water Risk Index to Improve Community Resilience," *IBM Journal of Research and Development*, Vol. 64, No. 1/2, 2020. As of June 15, 2020:
https://doi.org/10.1147/JRD.2019.2945301

Klimek, Peter, Sebastian Poledna, and Stefan Thurner, "Quantifying Economic Resilience from Input-Output Susceptibility to Improve Predictions of Economic Growth and Recovery," *Nature Communications*, Vol. 10, No. 1677, 2019, pp. 1–9.

Lenzen, M., R. Wood, and T. Wiedmann, "Uncertainty Analysis for Multi-Region Input-Output Models—a Case Study of the UK's Carbon Footprint," *Economic Systems Research*, Vol. 22, No. 1, 2010, pp. 43–63.

Leontief, Wassily W., "Input-Output Economics," *Scientific American*, Vol. 185, No. 4, 1951a, pp. 15–21.

———, *The Structure of the American Economy, 1919–1939*, 2nd ed., New York: Oxford University Press, 1951b.

———, *Input-Output Economics*, New York: Oxford University Press, 1966.

Lian, Chenyang, and Yacov Y. Haimes, "Managing the Risk of Terrorism to Interdependent Infrastructure Systems Through the Dynamic Inoperability Input-Output Model," *Systems Engineering*, Vol. 9, No. 3, 2006, pp. 241–258.

Lyles, Ward, Philip Berke, and Gavin Smith, "A Comparison of Local Hazard Mitigation Plan Quality in Six States," *Landscape and Urban Planning*, Vol. 122, 2014, pp. 89–99.

Madrigano, Jaime, Kazuhiko Ito, Sarah Johnson, Patrick L. Kinney, and Thomas Matte, "A Case-Only Study of Vulnerability to Heat Wave–Related Mortality in New York City (2000–2011)," *Environmental Health Perspectives*, Vol. 123, No. 7, 2015, pp. 672–678.

Marten, Alex L., and Richard Garbaccio, *An Applied General Equilibrium Model for the Analysis of Environmental Policy: SAGE v1.0 Technical Documentation*, working paper, U.S. Environmental Protection Agency National Center for Environmental Economics, 2018. As of June 15, 2020:
https://www.epa.gov/sites/production/files/2018-10/documents/2018-05.pdf

Maru, Yiheyis Taddele, Mark Stafford Smith, Ashley Sparrow, Patricia F. Pinho, and Opha Pauline Dube, "A Linked Vulnerability and Resilience Framework for Adaptation Pathways in Remote Disadvantaged Communities," *Global Environmental Change*, Vol. 28, 2014, pp. 337–350.

Maslow, Abraham Harold, "A Theory of Human Motivation," *Psychological Review*, Vol. 50, No. 4, 1943, p. 370.

Miller, Ronald E., and Peter D. Blair, *Input Output Analysis: Foundations and Extensions*, 2nd ed., New York: Cambridge University Press, 2009.

Mobley, William, Kayode O. Atoba, and Wesley E. Highfield, "Uncertainty in Flood Mitigation Practices: Assessing the Economic Benefits of Property Acquisition and Elevation in Flood-Prone Communities," *Sustainability*, Vol. 12, No. 5, 2020, p. 2098.

Moser, Susanne C., and Julia Ekstrom, "A Framework to Diagnose Barriers to Climate Change Adaptation," *Proceedings of the National Academy of Sciences of the United States of America*, Vol. 107, No. 51, December 2010, pp. 22026–22031.

Multihazard Mitigation Council, *Natural Hazard Mitigation Saves: 2018 Interim Report*, principal investigator: K. Porter; co–principal investigators C. Scawthorn and C. Huyck; investigators: R. Eguchi, Z. Hu, A. Reeder, and P. Schneider, director, Washington, D.C.: National Institute of Building Sciences, 2018. As of May 22, 2020:
https://cdn.ymaws.com/www.nibs.org/resource/resmgr/mmc/NIBS_MSv2-2018_Interim-Repor.pdf

National Fire Protection Association, "Public Education," webpage undated. As of May 21, 2020:
https://www.nfpa.org/Public-Education/Fire-causes-and-risks/Wildfire/Firewise-USA

National Institute of Standards and Technology, *Community Resilience | NIST*, June 18, 2020. As of June 19, 2020:
https://www.nist.gov/topics/community-resilience

National Research Council, *Disaster Resilience: A National Imperative*, Washington, D.C.: National Academies Press, 2012. As of June 15, 2020:
https://doi.org/10.17226/13457

National Weather Service, *Summary of Natural Hazard Statistics for 2017 in the United States*, April 2018. As of June 16, 2020:
https://www.weather.gov/media/hazstat/sum17.pdf

NIST, "Community Resilience," webpage, undated. As of June 15, 2020:
https://www.nist.gov/topics/community-resilience

Okuyama, Yasuhide, "Economic Modeling for Disaster Impact Analysis: Past, Present, and Future," *Economic Systems Research*, Vol. 19, No. 2, 2007, pp. 115–124.

Okuyama, Yasuhide, and Joost R. Santos, "Disaster Impact and Input-Output Analysis," *Economic Systems Research*, Vol. 26, No. 1, 2014, pp. 1–12. As of June 15, 2020:
https://doi.org/10.1080/09535314.2013.871505

Peacock, W., S. Brody, W. Seitz, W. Merrell, A. Vedlitz, S. Zahran, R. Harriss, and R. Stickney, *Advancing Resilience of Coastal Localities: Developing, Implementing, and Sustaining the Use of Coastal Resilience Indicators: A Final Report*, Hazard Reduction and Recovery Center, Texas A&M University, 2010.

Pelkmans, Jacques, Lourdes Acedo, and Alessandro Maravalle, "How Product Market Reforms Lubricate Shock Adjustment in the Euro Area," *European Economy Economic Papers*, No. 341, 2008. As of June 15, 2020:
https://ec.europa.eu/economy_finance/publications/pages/publication13205_en.pdf

Preston, B. L., E. J. Yuen, and R. M. Westaway, "Putting Vulnerability to Climate Change on the Map: A Review of Approaches, Benefits, and Risks," *Sustainability Science*, Vol. 6, No. 2, 2011, pp. 177–202.

Procurement Capacity Development Centre, Capacity Development Group, Bureau for Development Policy, United Nations Development Fund, *Public Procurement Capacity Development Guide*, New York, October 2010. As of December 10, 2019:
https://www.undp.org/content/dam/aplaws/publication/en/publications/capacity-development/undp-procurement-capacity-assessment-users-guide/Procurement%20Capacity%20Assessment%20Guide.pdf

Public Law 115-254, FAA Reauthorization Act of 2018, October 5, 2018.

Public Law 100-707, Robert T. Stafford Disaster Relief and Emergency Assistance Act, November 23, 1988.

Reid, C. E., M. S. O'Neill, C. J. Gronlund, S. J. Brines, D. G. Brown, and A. V. Diez-Roux, "Mapping Community Determinants of Heat Vulnerability," *Environmental Health Perspectives*, Vol. 117, No. 11, 2009, pp. 1730–1736.

Risk Steering Committee, *DHS Risk Lexicon*, Washington, D.C.: U.S. Department of Homeland Security, 2010. As of May 20, 2020:
https://www.dhs.gov/xlibrary/assets/dhs-risk-lexicon-2010.pdf

Roberts, Patrick S., *Disasters and the American State: How Politicians, Bureaucrats, and the Public Prepare for the Unexpected*, New York: Cambridge University Press, 2013.

Rose, Adam, J. Benavides, S. E. Chang, P. Szczesniak, and D. Lim, "The Regional Economic Impact of an Earthquake: Direct and Indirect Effects of Electricity Lifeline Disruptions," *Journal of Regional Science*, Vol. 37, No. 3 (1997), 437–458.

Rose, Adam, and Shu-Yi Liao, "Modeling Regional Economic Resilience to Disasters: A Computable General Equilibrium Analysis of Water Service Disruptions," *Journal of Regional Science*, Vol. 45, No. 1, 2005, pp. 75–112.

Rose, Adam, Gbadebo Oladosu, and Shu-Yi Liao, "Business Interruption Impacts of a Terrorist Attack on the Electric Power System of Los Angeles: Customer Resilience to a Total Blackout," *Risk Analysis*, Vol. 27, No. 3, 2007, pp. 513–531.

Rose, Adam, and Gauri-Shankar Guha, "Computable General Equilibrium Modeling of Electric Utility Lifeline Losses from Earthquakes," in Y. Okuyama and S. E. Chang, eds., *Modeling Spatial and Economic Impacts of Disasters: Advances in Spatial Science*, Berlin: Springer, 2004. As of June 15, 2020:
https://doi.org/10.1007/978-3-540-24787-6_7

Rose, Adam, Ian Su Wing, Dan Wei, and Misak Avetisyan, *Total Regional Economic Losses from Water Supply Disruptions to the Los Angeles County Economy*, final report to Los Angeles County Economic Development Corporation, USC, 2012. As of June 15, 2020:
https://www.laedc.org/reports/WaterSupplyDisruptionStudy_November2012.pdf

Round, Jeffery, "Social Accounting Matrices and SAM-Based Multiplier Analysis," in F. Bourguignon and L. Pereira da Silva, eds., *The Impact of Economic Policies on Poverty and Income Distribution: Evaluation Techniques and Tools*, Washington, D.C.: World Bank, 2003, pp. 261–276.

Rufat, S., E. Tate, C. G. Burton, and A. S. Maroof, "Social Vulnerability to Floods: Review of Case Studies and Implications for Measurement," *International Journal of Disaster Risk Reduction*, Vol. 14, 2015, pp. 470–486.

Sebald, C., *Towards an Integrated Flood Vulnerability Index—a Flood Vulnerability Assessment*, thesis, University of Southampton, 2010.

Smit, Barry, and Johanna Wandel, "Adaptation, Adaptive Capacity and Vulnerability," *Global Environmental Change*, Vol. 16, 2006, pp. 282–292.

Smith, Gavin, Ward Lyles, and Philip Berke, "The Role of the State in Building Local Capacity and Commitment for Hazard Mitigation Planning," *International Journal of Mass Emergencies and Disasters*, Vol. 31, No. 2, August 2013, pp. 178–203.

Soares, M. B., A. S. Gagnon, and R. M. Doherty, "Conceptual Elements of Climate Change Vulnerability Assessments: A Review," *International Journal of Climate Change Strategies and Management*, Vol. 4, No. 1, 2012, pp. 6–35.

Spader, Jonathan, and Jennifer Turnham, "CDBG Disaster Recovery Assistance and Homeowners' Rebuilding Outcomes Following Hurricanes Katrina and Rita," *Housing Policy Debate*, Vol. 24, January 2014, pp. 213–237.

Stahmer, C., "Social Accounting Matrices and Extended Input-Output Tables," in OECD, *Measuring Sustainable Development: Integrated Economic, Environmental and Social Frameworks*, Paris: OECD, 2004, pp. 313–344.

Strong, Aaron, and Debra Knopman, *Landscape Survey to Support Flood Apex National Flood Decision Support Toolbox: Definitions and Existing Tools*, Santa Monica, Calif.: RAND Corporation, RR-1933-UNC, 2017. As of November 22, 2019:
https://www.rand.org/pubs/research_reports/RR1933.html

Tatano, Hirokazu, and Satoshi Tsuchiya, "A Framework for Economic Loss Estimation Due to Seismic Transportation Network Disruption: A Spatial Computable General Equilibrium Approach," *Natural Hazards*, Vol. 44, 2008, pp. 253–265. As of June 15, 2020:
https://doi.org/10.1007/s11069-007-9151-0

Tate, E., "Social Vulnerability Indices: A Comparative Assessment Using Uncertainty and Sensitivity Analysis," *Natural Hazards*, Vol. 63, No. 2, 2012, pp. 325–347.

Tate, E., A. Strong, T. Kraus, and H. Xiong, "Flood Recovery and Property Acquisition in Cedar Rapids, Iowa," *Natural Hazards*, Vol. 80, No. 3, 2016, pp. 2055–2079.

United Nations Capital Development Fund, *Delivering the Goods: Building Local Government Capacity to Achieve the Millennium Development Goals*, New York, June 2007. As of November 26, 2019:
https://www.local2030.org/library/96/Delivering-the-Goods
—Building-Local-Government-Capacity-to-Achieve-the-Millennium-Development-Goals.pdf

United Nations Development Programme, *Capacity Assessment Methodology User's Guide*, New York, November 2008. As of November 27, 2019:
https://www.undp.org/content/dam/aplaws/publication/en/publications/capacity-development/undp-capacity-assessment-methodology/UNDP%20Capacity%20Assessment%20Users%20Guide.pdf

U.S. Agency for International Development, *Human and Institutional Capacity Development Handbook*, August 2011. As of November 27, 2019:
https://usaidlearninglab.org/sites/default/files/resource/files/HICD%20Handbook%202011%20-%2008.pdf

U.S. Bureau of Labor Statistics, "Consumer Price Index," webpage, undated. As of May 22, 2020:
https://www.bls.gov/cpi/

———, "Quarterly Census of Employment and Wages: QCEW Location Quotient Details," last updated May 13, 2020. As of May 28, 2020:
https://www.bls.gov/cew/about-data/location-quotients-explained.htm

U.S. Census Bureau, "U.S. Cities Are Home to 62.7 Percent of the U.S. Population, but Comprise Just 3.5 Percent of Land Area," press release CB15-33, Washington, D.C., March 4, 2015. As of May 6, 2020:
https://www.census.gov/newsroom/press-releases/2015/cb15-33.html

U.S. Code, Title 42, Section 5133, Predisaster Hazard Mitigation, January 3, 2012. As of May 20, 2020:
https://www.law.cornell.edu/uscode/text/42/5133

U.S. Environmental Protection Agency, *Development of a Climate Resilience Screening Index (CRSI): An Assessment of Resilience to Acute Meteorological Events and Selected Natural Hazards*, October 2017. As of May 19, 2020:
https://nepis.epa.gov/Exe/ZyPDF.cgi?Dockey=P100SSN6.txt

U.S. Geological Survey, "Earthquake Hazards," webpage, undated. As of May 20, 2020:
https://www.usgs.gov/natural-hazards/earthquake-hazards/earthquakes

Vasseur, Michael, Dwayne M. Butler, Brandon Crosby, Benjamin N. Harris, and Christopher Scott Adams, *An Assessment of the Joint Requirements Council's (JRC) Organization and Staffing*, Homeland Security Operational Analysis Center operated by the RAND Corporation, RR-2473-DHS, 2018. As of March 17, 2020:
https://www.rand.org/pubs/research_reports/RR2473.html

Weber, C. L., "Uncertainties in Constructing Environmental Multiregional Input-Output Models," International Input-Output Meeting on Managing the Environment, Seville, Spain, July 9–11, 2008. As of June 15, 2020:
http://www.upo.es/econ/IIOMME08/index.php

Wing, Ian Sue, "Computable General Equilibrium Models for the Analysis of Energy and Climate Policies," in Joanne Evans and Lester C. Hunt, eds., *International Handbook on the Economics of Energy*, Cheltanham, UK: Edward Elgar, 2009, pp. 332–366.

Wing, Ian, Adam Rose, and Anne Wein, "Economic Consequence Analysis of the ARkStorm Scenario," *Natural Hazards Review*, Vol. 17, 2015. As of June 15, 2020:
https://doi.org/10.1061/(ASCE)NH.1527-6996.0000173